A Dad After God's Own Heart

JIM GEORGE

HARVEST HOUSE PUBLISHERS
EUGENE, OREGON

Cover by Garborg Design Works, Savage, Minnesota

Cover photos © warrengoldswain, BlueOrange Studio / Bigstock

A DAD AFTER GOD'S OWN HEART
Copyright © 2014 by Jim George
Published by Harvest House Publishers
Eugene, Oregon 97402
www.harvesthousepublishers.com

Library of Congress Cataloging-in-Publication Data
George, Jim, 1943-
A dad after God's own heart / Jim George.
    pages cm
ISBN 978-0-7369-5087-9 (pbk.)
ISBN 978-0-7369-5088-6 (eBook)
1. Fatherhood—Religious aspects—Christianity. I. Title.
BV4529.17.G46 2014
248.8'421—dc23

2013037698

14 15 16 17 18 19 20 21 22 / BP-CD / 10 9 8 7 6 5 4 3 2 1

*This book is dedicated to dads everywhere
who are doing their best with God's help
to be the best dads they can be.
This especially includes my two sons-in-law,
Paul Seitz and Paul Zaengle,
who are faithfully training my eight grandchildren
in the instruction of the Lord.*

Contents

From a Dad's Heart

Dear Dad,

At last! After having written books on being a *man* after God's own heart and a *husband* after God's own heart, I have finally written one about being a *dad* after God's own heart. And I want to alert you right away that I didn't write it because I'm an expert on parenting or because I was always successful as a father. In fact, *trying* to be a good dad is where my journey toward becoming a good dad began.

One day at age 30, I woke up, looked at my two little daughters just a year apart in age, and realized I didn't have a clue about what it meant to be God's kind of dad. Fortunately, about that time, I had started reading my Bible and was beginning to get some idea of what was required of a father.

Next I found several men in my church who agreed to help me understand and fulfill my role as a dad. After several decades of growing spiritually, I wrote the two books I mentioned a moment ago—one for men, and one for husbands. I even wrote books for teen and tween guys[1] about their priorities. But I remained hesitant to write a book on being a dad. You see, the jury was still out on my parenting. Were my efforts fruitful? Were my grown-up girls walking with the Lord and raising their own children to love God too?

Finally, after seeing my own children spiritually strong, walking with the Lord, and pointing their eight little ones toward God, I felt it was now okay to write about being a dad after God's own heart.

Friend and fellow dad, it's been 30 years since my wake-up call about my God-given responsibilities for my two little girls. That's 30 years of learning how I could give my best to applying God's principles for parents, 30 years of fervent prayer, and 30 years of discovering what being a dad after God's own heart requires.

Being a Dad After God's Own Heart...

...*requires time.* How much time does it take for an acorn to become a tall, sturdy oak tree? Years—in fact, decades! Parenting takes daily time for a lifetime. Daily teaching and training must be continuous and purposeful as you invest your life into raising children after God's own heart.

...*requires personal commitment.* The most effective modeling comes with a close relationship between parent and child. There is little impact without contact. Discipleship requires personal involvement. The closer your relationship with your child is, the more effective the training—and the greater the impact.

...*requires perseverance.* There are no quick fixes when it comes to being God's kind of dad. Rather than being a series of short-term solutions to child-raising, a dad's role is a multifaceted relationship that lasts a lifetime.

...*requires focus.* Effective parenting is not a casual undertaking. It takes being a faithful dad, submitting yourself to God's instructions, and actively seeking to bring up your children according to biblical principles.

...*requires planning.* Success doesn't just happen. You either plan to be a good dad and go for it, or you end up with whatever happens. If you don't plan a path for your children to walk, others will be glad to take control of their minds and futures.

...*requires a team effort.* Parenting is a team sport. If you're married, your wife, the mother of your children, is the first and best resource you have to assist you in your desire to be a solid, proactive dad. Beyond your wife, you have your church, the youth leaders in your church, and maybe some godly grandparents. Allow them to assist you, but realize that *you* are the one who is ultimately responsible to God for your children.

...*reaps the greatest of blessings.* "Children are a heritage from the LORD...happy is the man who has his quiver full of them" (Psalm 127:3,5). A father experiences "no greater joy than to hear that [his] children walk in truth" (3 John 4).

This book is not the final answer to all your parenting problems or difficulties. It's actually more of a guide for *you* as you grow into a spiritually mature man and equip yourself to model spiritual truths for your children. To help you with these goals, at the end of this book you'll find a daily Bible reading schedule and a brief guide titled "How to Study the Bible." I've also included study questions to help you dig a little deeper into your role of father. You can do this in your quiet time or with a few other dads or in your men's study group.

You can do it, Dad. You can be a dad after God's own heart. How can I say that? Because "His divine power has given to us all things that pertain to life and godliness" (2 Peter 1:3). God will be with you all the way, giving you wisdom that is from above, strength that enables you to do all things (including be a great dad), and a love for your children that knows no bounds. I'm praying for you!

Yours for the Master,

Jim George

We can never afford to forget that we teach our children
to call God father, and the only conception of fatherhood
that they can have is the conception which we give them.
Human fatherhood should be molded and modeled on
the pattern of the fatherhood of God. It is the tremendous
duty of the human father to be as good a father as God.[1]

WILLIAM BARCLAY

A Dad Who Has a Divine Model

Grace to you and peace from God our Father.

1 CORINTHIANS 1:3

Greg had assumed a posture that wasn't all that familiar—he was on his knees. He had just come from the hospital, where he had just experienced the birth of his first child, a baby girl he and his wife had named Mary Lou. The reason for including *Mary* in her name was because his wife, Margaret, had once had a little sister by that name. Tragically, this sister had died of cancer at a young age.

Now, after the birth and initial celebration, Greg had staggered home feeling quite tired. He had gotten very little sleep, and he was hoping to get some rest before going back to the hospital. The way he was feeling, you would have thought he had been the one in labor all those hours. Maybe it was the lack of sleep, or the impact of seeing that new little life, but whatever it was, Greg was overwhelmed by the prospect of being a new dad. Only now, after the months of anticipation, was Greg feeling the gravity of his new role and responsibility. He was a dad!

So, as he knelt with his arms leaning on a kitchen chair, Greg prayed, "God, I don't have a clue of what it means to be a father, a dad, or a parent to little Mary Lou. I need help. Please guide me each step of the way as I assume my new role." Then Greg went on to pray his way through little Mary Lou's life from infancy all the way through marriage!

As Greg got up off his knees, he felt like a reassuring celestial hand was resting on his shoulder. He believed his prayer had been heard and that God would be faithful to give him the wisdom he needed to be a good dad.

Greg felt that he had just entered into a partnership with God. If he was faithful to do his part, Greg knew God was there to lead him through the process of becoming a dad after God's own heart.

As a brand new dad, Greg was concerned about being a father. He was operating in a vacuum. He had no good role models. His dad had been killed in a car accident when he was seven, and his mother had continually made wrong choices with the men she had married since then. Greg could think of very few, if any, actions or attitudes exhibited by any of these men that could be of help in raising little Mary Lou. He shuddered to think where he would have been if Jesus hadn't entered his life and transformed him into a child of God.

Why is it that for many of us, it takes a major event to provide a wake-up call for spiritual growth? For Greg it was the responsibility of a first child. For others, it may be the death of someone close, or a divorce or a disabling condition. Greg got his wake-up call, and thankfully, he has begun to start thinking in the right direction. But how? How—and where—is he going to find a model of what a father should look and act like?

The Impact of a Role Model

The effects of nearly 20 years of growing up under a parent (for our purposes, a dad) will leave a lasting impression on a child. The imprint of that modeling isn't always visible, but the results of a father's influence will show up in the child at some point in the future. If Dad had an anger problem, guess what? His children will have trouble containing their anger. If Dad physically abused his children, guess what? The next generation of moms and dads will most likely treat their own children the same way. Or, as an overreaction, they may go to the other extreme and completely withhold discipline of any kind whatsoever.

Even in the Bible we don't find a lot of good human role models for dads. So let me make my point with a classic negative role model in a dad named Eli.

In Eli we see a case of "like father, like sons." Eli was a priest of Israel during the last days of the Judges (1 Samuel 2). As a priest, he was allowed to take a portion of certain offerings from the people for his services to them. Unfortunately, he abused this privilege and took more than his portion. Here is God's indictment of Eli:

> Why do you scorn my sacrifices and offerings? Why
> do you give your sons more honor than you give me—
> for you and they have become fat from the best offer-
> ings of my people Israel! (1 Samuel 2:29 NLT).

Did you notice the connection between father and sons? God spelled it out: "You and they have become fat from the best offerings of my people Israel." Eli was guilty of taking more of the sacrifice than he was allotted, which had made him fat. He was guilty of despising the offerings the people were giving to the Lord. And guess what? Eli's boys were following in their dad's footsteps (see 2:12-17).

> Now the sons of Eli were corrupt; they did not know
> the Lord. And the priests' custom with the people was
> that when any man offered a sacrifice, the priest's ser-
> vant would come with a three-pronged fleshhook in
> his hand while the meat was boiling. Then he would
> thrust it into the [cooking vessel]...and the priest
> would take for himself all that the fleshhook brought
> up. So they did in Shiloh to all the Israelites who came
> there (verses 12-14).

For a priest to take part of the offering was permitted. But the sons of Eli went beyond what was prescribed by the Law of Moses and demanded meat from the people before they cooked it. If the people balked, Eli's sons would say, "No, but you must give it now; and if not, I will take it by force" (verse 16). God did not take this offense lightly: "The sin of the young men was very great before the

LORD, for men abhorred the offering of the LORD" (verse 17). Tragically, Eli was a participant in this, for as God said, "You give your
sons more honor than you give me" (1 Samuel 2:29 NLT).

What a chilling thought to realize that your children are observing your life, logging your activities, and repeating your actions,
whether good or bad. I know from personal experience that what
I observed from my own father's behavior served as both a positive
and negative influence on my role as a husband and father. Modeling is truly a powerful force!

God, Our Father

Are you beginning to understand the importance of presenting
the right kind of model for your children? And are you wondering
where can you find this right kind of model? The Bible is an obvious
first place to look. Hopefully, your spiritual understanding is much
further along than Greg's. Unlike Greg, you may be aware of what
the Bible says about the model you have in your loving, caring, giving, and guiding Father in heaven. The Bible presents many verses
about what a strong, consistent model you have in God the Father.
And you are doubly blessed if you have an earthly father who has
also provided a constant model of godly fatherhood.

But for those of us who don't have this kind of legacy to fall
back on, we, like Greg, are forced to look around for others who can
model what a father should be for his children. So where do we start?

Of course, the first place is your Bible. There, you find that God
is the ultimate model of what it means to be a father.

God is often spoken of as "the
Father" in the Bible. He is called "the
Father of our Lord Jesus Christ" (Ephesians 3:14). Probably the most famous
reference to God as Father came in the
most famous of prayers uttered by Jesus
Himself. Jesus began this prayer by saying, "Our Father in heaven,
hallowed be Your name" (Matthew 6:9).

**God is the ultimate model of
what it means to be a father.**

God the Father is a person; therefore, He has character qualities
that theologians refer to as *attributes*. These attributes are what identify and distinguish who God is as a person.

Some of God's characteristics belong only to Him, such as His infinity, eternity, immutability, omnipresence, omniscience, and sovereignty. These qualities cannot be passed on to His creation. But other characteristics, like love, truth, holiness, patience, and kindness, can—at least in a limited sense—be found in man, who was created in God's image. These are called the "communicable" qualities of God because they can be expressed by man. And hopefully that includes you and me as dads.

The Father of Those Who Believe

Having God as your heavenly Father and emulating His attributes to your children presupposes that you are His child. As the saying goes, You can't impart what you do not possess.

To be personally related to God as your Father can only come through putting your faith and trust in His Son, the Lord Jesus Christ. This has to be the starting point in your quest to be a dad after God's own heart.

If you are not a child of the Father, it's going to be difficult for you to live out His character before your children. Oh, you can still be a decent dad without God's help, but without God's character abiding in you, being a dad after God's own heart just isn't possible.

So if you truly desire to be God's kind of a dad, then now is the time to make sure you have access to God's power through a relationship with Him. To do that you need to think about your sin, because sin is what separates you from a holy God. *Sin* is anything that you do that misses God's perfect standard of holy behavior. Have you ever told just one lie, even "a little white lie"? According to Scripture, whoever attempts to keep all of God's law "yet stumbles at just one point is guilty of breaking all of it" (James 2:10). And we are told in Romans 3 that "there is none righteous; no, not one... there is none who does good; no, not one" (verses 10,12). This means all of us. Everyone has sinned and fallen short of what God calls for.

But there is hope! The Bible gives clear instructions on how to deal with your sin. So if you are a new dad like Greg or a seasoned veteran who truly wants God's help in raising your children, then read these verses from the Bible. They form what is called "the Roman Road" toward a relationship with God the Father because all these verses come out of the book of Romans. Follow what the apostle Paul says as he leads you down the Romans Road toward salvation through the Father's Son, Jesus Christ:

Romans 3:23—"All have sinned and fall short of the glory of God."

We were "all" born with sin. You might not want to admit it, but you have sin in your heart. You are under the power of sin's control. Oh, maybe you do a few good things in your life, but unless you are perfect, you are still a sinner. Step 1 for you is to admit that you are a sinner.

Romans 6:23a—"The wages of sin is death."

Sin is a dead-end street. It ends in spiritual "death." We all face physical death. But spiritual death is worse because it separates you from God for all eternity. The Bible teaches that there is a place called the lake of fire, where lost people will be in torment forever. It is the place where people who are spiritually dead will go. Step 2 for you is to understand that you deserve not only physical death, but also spiritual death for your sin.

Romans 6:23b—"But the gift of God is eternal life in Christ Jesus our Lord."

Notice the little word "but" in the line above. There is an answer to your sin problem. Salvation is a free "gift" from God to you! You can't earn this gift; rather, you must reach out and receive it. Step 3 for you is to ask God to forgive you and save you.

Romans 5:8—"God demonstrates His own love toward us, in that while we were still sinners, Christ died for us."

When Jesus died on the cross, He paid sin's penalty. He paid the price for all sin, and when He took all the sins of the world on Himself on the cross, He bought—He purchased—you out of slavery to sin and death. The only requirement is to believe in Jesus and what He has done for you. Jesus did all this because He loved you. Step 4 for you is to give your life to God the Father through Jesus Christ, His Son.

Romans 10:9-10—"If you confess with your mouth the Lord Jesus and believe in your heart that God has raised Jesus from the dead, you will be saved."

If you've already done all of the above, thank God and live for Him! If you have put your faith and trust in Jesus as your Savior, you are a child of God, and God is your Father. And, as a bonus, you can be an outstanding model of a believer in Christ. Strive to live a life of obedience to His commands, and you will be a dad after God's own heart.

You Can Do It, Dad!

If you are a dad, you are part of an exciting exclusive club. However you came to be your children's dad and whatever the circumstances, you are their dad. Being a father is one of the greatest privileges God extends to you.

But this role also bears the greatest of responsibilities. Your children are yours to influence for good or evil. Your example will mark them for life. Maybe you need to do like our friend Greg did—get down on your knees and ask God to give you His wisdom to do whatever is necessary to be a dad after God's own heart. And even better is to do this every day.

Small Steps That Make a Big Difference

1. *Love your wife.* The most important step you can take as a dad is to love your wife. This may not be your easiest step. But it will be the one that goes the farthest in modeling God the Father's love for His children.

2. *Affirm in your heart that you are in the faith—that you are in Christ.* If you are, you have access to all the help you will ever need to be God's kind of dad.

3. *Make sure you are growing spiritually.* God wants you to "grow in the grace and knowledge of our Lord and Savior Jesus Christ" (2 Peter 3:18). Because spiritual growth is a command, that means you have a choice. If you want to be a dad after God's own heart, you will want to choose to grow spiritually. So carve out some time each day to spend with your heavenly Father.

4. *Don't make excuses for not reading your Bible.* Getting into God's Word is an obvious step for all things spiritual—including being a dad. I've heard a lot of men say, "I have to be at work really early." Or "I don't understand the Bible." Or "I don't know where to start." Yet if something is truly important to you, you'll find a way to fit it into your busy schedule, and you'll take time to learn how to do it. Not only does a Christian man, husband, and father *need* to spend time with God daily, but he should *want* to.

To the child, the father is God's representative;
this makes the father's task sacred and serious.
We fathers are to deal with our children
as God deals with us.[2]

JOHN DRESCHER

One night a father overheard his son pray:
Dear God, make me the kind of man my Daddy is.
Later that night, the father prayed, Dear God, make me
the kind of man my son wants me to be.

AUTHOR UNKNOWN

A Dad Who Walks in the Spirit

I say then: Walk in the Spirit,
and you shall not fulfill the lust of the flesh.

GALATIANS 5:16

Previously we left Greg mulling over the prospects of finding a model to pattern his life after. Because of his budding-but-baby level of spiritual maturity, Greg didn't realize what resources he already possessed as a Christian—resources that could make him a great dad. But as he pulled into the hospital parking lot with a carload of balloons for the baby and chocolates for his wife, he was ready to do whatever was necessary to become a dad after God's own heart. Greg couldn't wait to tell his wife about his spiritual breakthrough. And when he did, she was thrilled about this newfound spark of spiritual interest. As the two of them talked, Margaret suggested that maybe one of the older men at church—like Bill Wilson—might be able to give Greg some direction.

As he thought about it, Greg liked this idea a lot. Yes, their church was definitely a place to start looking for help with learning about being a dad after God's own heart. Greg was a little sad when he realized he should have had this wake-up call long ago, but he was excited that he was now on the right track. Thank goodness his little Mary Lou was only one day old!

Greg planned to call Bill Wilson immediately to see if he could start meeting with him. He could hardly wait to begin the process of a "manly spiritual makeover."

The Father's Gift of the Son

If you attend a church, chances are you'll find men there who can serve as excellent role models for learning how to be a godly dad. It probably won't take you long to pick these men out of the crowd. They wear their role well. New dads and dads who need help and advice can go to these men and learn from their insights, experiences, and yes, even their mistakes. But while you are looking for these real-life models, don't forget that your ultimate example of fatherhood is God the Father. He is and always will be your supreme role model.

Just as your children possess part of your essence—your DNA—you as a new creation in Christ possess God's presence in you. As a believer, God's Holy Spirit dwells in you (Romans 8:9; Ephesians 1:14). The Holy Spirit's job is to teach and guide us (John 14:26). It is the Holy Spirit who gives you the ability to be a godly model for your children. He gives you all the spiritual resources you need to be God's kind of dad. This internal power will exhibit itself in what is called "the fruit of the Spirit." This fruit is described as godly character qualities in Galatians 5:22-23: "The fruit of the Spirit is love, joy, peace, longsuffering, kindness, goodness, faithfulness, gentleness, self-control."

The Fruit of the Spirit

Throughout the Bible, "fruit" refers to the external evidence of what is within. Any person who has received Jesus as Savior has the Lord living within, and that indwelling of God's Holy Spirit will evidence itself as good "fruit"—the "fruits of righteousness" (Philippians 1:11). Here are a few facts about the fruit of the Spirit:

- —This godly behavior is expressed as love, joy, peace, patience, kindness, goodness, faithfulness, gentleness, and self-control.

- —Every fruit of the Spirit is commanded in Scripture. "Walk by the Spirit" (Galatians 5:16).

- —Every fruit, therefore, because it is commanded, requires a decision, a choice. Will you or won't you "walk in the Spirit"? If you choose to do so, "you shall not fulfill the lust of the flesh" (5:16).

— Every fruit of the Spirit is illustrated in the life of Christ. Walking by the Spirit means being controlled by the Spirit, acting like Jesus. Jesus walked moment by moment in and by the Spirit; therefore, His life habitually and totally exhibited godly behavior. He loved perfectly, He lived in constant joy, and so on.

This godly behavior, or fruit of the Spirit, is what your children can expect from you and will see in you when you are walking with Jesus and following the Spirit's leading. It's like this: Your children can't see Jesus, but they can see you. From you, they can learn what Jesus is like. Are you acting like Christ?

Here's what your life will look like when you are walking in the Spirit:

You will exhibit love—Love is self-sacrifice. This simple definition crystalizes what the Bible teaches about love. "Love is not an emotion. It is an act of sacrificing self. It is not necessarily feeling love toward a particular person. It may not have any emotion connected with it."[1] Here's how the Bible describes love: "God demonstrates His own love toward us, in that while we were still sinners, Christ died for us" (Romans 5:8). From this verse we see no emotion, but we definitely see that God's love involved sacrifice.

This is a book about you as a dad, and your role in the lives of your children. If you want to be a successful father, then the first person who should receive the overflow of your love for God is your wife. If she knows that she is your first love after God, then you and your wife will model God's kind of marital love to your children.

God's kind of love is not the love portrayed by the world. The world's kind of love is usually defined in terms of emotions, and is frequently fickle depending on our feelings. It is conditional and says, "If you love me, then I'll love you." It's also transitory, for it says, "I don't love you anymore," or "I've fallen out of love with you."

By contrast, God's kind of love is unconditional. It says, "I love you regardless." It's a love that is steadfast no matter what.

When a dad is walking by the Spirit, his love is enduring, impartial, and willing to sacrifice for the good of his children. His love isn't just an emotion; he will show his love through his actions:

What man is there among you who, if his son asks for bread, will give him a stone? Or if he asks for a fish, will he give him a serpent? If you then, being evil, know how to give good gifts to your children, how much more will your Father who is in heaven give good things to those who ask Him! (Matthew 7:9-11).

Dad, yours is to be a love that willingly sacrifices yourself for your children. This love may even require at some point the ultimate sacrifice of your life for them. But for now, God is asking you to be a daily living sacrifice for your children. For example, love will sacrifice a round of golf with the guys or watching The Big Game on TV to attend a son's ball game or a daughter's recital. When you put your children first, you will make a tremendous impression on them.

You will exhibit joy—When life is good, things are going well on the job, and the problems are few at home, praise and thanksgiving flow freely from your heart and lips. When the sun is shining brightly in your life, you are *happy*. But when life turns black and stormy, praise and thanksgiving don't flow quite so easily. This is where people get confused about the distinction between *spiritual joy* and the human emotion of *happiness*.

> When you put your children first, you will make a tremendous impression on them.

Happiness is an emotion you have when you are experiencing good fortune and success. *Spiritual joy*, however, is what you experience when you choose to follow God's advice and "in everything give thanks" (1 Thessalonians 5:18) no matter what happens—even when things go wrong. A more accurate definition of *joy* is "the sacrifice of praise."

Like love, joy is a sacrifice. Even in the times when you don't feel like praising God or thanking Him, when you commit to doing what God says in spite of your circumstances, you will experience joy. That's why it's called a *sacrifice*. During the times when you would rather stay stuck in your anger or discouragement, inner joy enables you to choose to look beyond your pain and make your praise a sacrifice to God.

Dad, ultimately the difference is this: Worldly happiness is based on your circumstances. And it's easy to let circumstances affect you to the point that when you walk through the front door of your home, your poor family doesn't know what to expect. Depending on how your day went, sometimes you walk through the door happy…and other times you walk through the door in a lousy mood. Commit yourself to sacrificing your attitudes and disappointments and walking through that door filled with the Spirit's joy. God's joy is in no way affected by what happens at the office. Your family will always look forward to your homecoming when you arrive with Christ's attitude of joy.

You will have peace—Peace is defined as "the sacrifice of trust." You and I make the sacrifice of trust when we face pain and stress in our lives and choose to trust God instead of stressing out. When circumstances in your life tempt you to worry or be filled with dread, you can choose to either give in to these responses, or place your trust in God. You can ask the Lord to fill you with His peace, or you can let anxiety fill your heart.

Do you know what happens when you choose to make the sacrifice of trust even in the midst of tremendous chaos? The apostle Paul describes the results:

> Be anxious for nothing, but in everything by prayer
> and supplication, with thanksgiving, let your requests
> be made known to God; and the peace of God, which
> surpasses all understanding, will guard your hearts and
> minds through Christ Jesus (Philippians 4:6-7).

Dad, I know you recognize that your job as a father to your children is incredibly important—yet also incredibly difficult. God is asking you to be a rock of strength and calmness regardless of what's happening to you and your family. When things get rough, many dads bolt and run away or delegate many of their duties to their wives. But when you do that, you fail to be the role model God has called you to be. The right response, then, is to trust God to give you His wisdom and resources in your time of need. Then when the crises arrive, your trust in the grace of God will give you the peace of God.

You will exhibit patience—Another of the characteristics of walking in the Spirit is patience. God's Word instructs you to "clothe yourselves with...patience" (Colossians 3:12 NIV). Patience is choosing to wait and do nothing. It has the ability to wait and wait for a long time!

Patience is a key to harmony in parenting relationships. It is a practical first step to getting along with the people under your own roof. Patience is a tall order—for example, you have to choose to wait before overreacting to the behavior of your children. That doesn't mean you won't eventually do something about their behavior. It just means your first response is to wait and make sure you make the right choice about how to respond. To show patience is to exhibit Christlike conduct.

You will exhibit kindness—While your patience waits and does nothing sinful (like get unreasonably mad, yell in anger, or kick the dog), kindness now plans for godly action. Like all the other fruit of the Spirit, kindness desires godly action and looks for opportunities to do something constructive. From a human standpoint this may not sound too manly, but Spirit-filled kindness is concerned about people. It's a matter of the heart.

Every time you show care for the well-being of your children, you demonstrate kindness. As a parent, you have a responsibility to train and discipline and correct your children's behavior. And a dad after God's own heart will make sure he disciplines out of kindness. To do that is an indicator you are filled with the Spirit. Spewing out threats, yelling, making rash statements, putting your children down or belittling them, and inflicting physical punishment that harms your children are all deeds of the flesh. These responses are a sure indicator that you are sinning. When you are filled with the Holy Spirit, your actions will reflect Christlikeness. Your kind, calm actions and wisdom marked by genuine, loving concern will show that you are a dad after God's own heart.

You will exhibit goodness—Goodness does everything it can to help others. It follows through on the concerns of kindness. Goodness takes the giant step from good intentions to actually doing everything it can to serve others. John Wesley, a famous preacher from the past, understood this principle of doing everything. In fact, he is said to have chosen to make it a rule for his life, and determine that he would make every effort to put the following words into practice.

> Do all the good you can,
> by all the means you can,
> in all the ways you can,
> in all the places you can,
> in all the times you can,
> to all the people you can,
> as long as ever you can.[2]

As a father, you have a legacy to leave behind. Can you imagine your children's every thought of you being the memory that you always had their best in your mind and did them good all the days of your life?

You will exhibit faithfulness—*Faithfulness* means choosing to do what you should do no matter what. Every day brings opportunities to do something you don't necessarily want to do. But faithfulness will do it regardless of feelings, moods, or desires. Doing what? Whatever it takes to be God's kind of dad. "Do it!" must become your battle cry as you struggle daily with your areas of weakness. For many men, tiredness heads the list. For others, it's laziness. But when you make a decision to do what you should, and you look to God for His strength and purpose in doing it, He will give you everything you need to have victory over tiredness, laziness, or any other challenge that comes your way.

Do you realize that faithfulness is a great rarity in our world? When you choose to be faithful, you exhibit the power of the Holy Spirit to a watching world—and especially your watching kids. Being faithful means choosing to get up each day and put on your "fathering" clothes regardless of how you feel. It means choosing to be a dad after God's own heart, with all its responsibilities, for one more day.

You will exhibit gentleness—Gentleness, or meekness, requires that you trust God. Therefore, gentleness chooses to "take it." Gentleness doesn't mean weakness, but actually has the idea of "strength under control." A man who is characterized by gentleness is willing to endure unkind behavior and suffering. He places His full trust in God's wisdom, power, and love. In the eyes of the world, gentleness may look like weakness, but it actually shows the greatest kind of strength!

When you act in gentleness, you exhibit Christlike character. Jesus Himself said, "Blessed are the gentle [humble, meek], for they shall inherit the earth" (Matthew 5:5 NASB). Then He proceeded to live out this meek and gentle spirit. In fact, He described Himself as "gentle and lowly in heart" (Matthew 11:29). Remember the first time you held your firstborn child? You were oh-so-careful with that new little person. That same attitude and care is still needed for each of your children no matter what their age. They still need the gentle touch of a loving dad.

You will exhibit self-control—In times of temptation, a man who walks by the Spirit chooses to "don't do it!" In other words, you don't give in to wrong emotions, to cravings, to urges. You choose not to think or do what you know is against God's Word. You choose not to excuse or baby yourself. You refuse to take the easy way out. You don't rationalize your wrong cravings in an attempt to make them legitimate. Rather, you resolve to say, "No!"—no to wrong thoughts, attitudes, and behaviors, including those in the sexual realm.

> **Don't start your day until you are committed to being controlled by the Spirit.**

Your determination to avoid thoughts or actions that dishonor Christ, shame your wife, and alienate your children should be ever constant. Satan would like nothing better than to destroy your family through your lapses in good moral judgment. Don't start your day until you are committed to being controlled by the Spirit. Your family needs your godly example, your self-control. "Don't do it."

The Art of Walking

Now that you've got a basic understanding of the fruit of the Spirit, what does it mean to "walk in the Spirit"? In simple terms, walking in the Spirit means living each moment in submission to

God. It means seeking to please God with the thoughts you choose to think, the words you choose to say, and the actions you choose to take. Walking in the Spirit means wanting to do the right thing and letting God guide you each step of the way.

Unfortunately, as you and I both realize, walking in the Spirit isn't easy. I'm sure you've noticed that as a believer in Christ, you still struggle with sin. Even the apostle Paul—who did mighty things in his many years of service for God—struggled. He confessed, "I know that nothing good dwells in me, that is, in my flesh; for the willing is present in me, but the doing of the good is not" (Romans 7:18 NASB). So what's the solution? In three words: *abide in Christ*.

To abide in Christ means to remain or stay near to Him. A Christian will abide in Christ—He will stay near to Jesus and will bear spiritual fruit for Jesus. Here is how Jesus Himself put it: "I am the vine, you are the branches. He who abides in Me, and I in him, bears much fruit; for without Me you can do nothing" (John 15:5). Abiding requires some choices:

Choosing to spend time in God's Word is one step—actually Step 1—you can take every day to abide in Christ. "The word of God is living and powerful, and sharper than any two-edged sword" (Hebrews 4:12). No other literature in the world has the power and force that's available to you in your Bible.

Choosing to spend time in prayer is another act that makes it possible for you to commune with Christ and abide in Him. You cannot keep your distance from Jesus if you are talking to Him! Prayer is a vital link between you and God. Just as a umbilical cord is a fetus's lifeline to its mother, prayer is your lifeline for maintaining an active relationship with Jesus. To abide in Christ and be a dad after God's own heart—a dad who walks with God—do all you can to strengthen your prayer life.

Choosing to obey God's commands also enhances your quest to abide in Christ. Obedience was an essential part of Jesus' own constant communion with the Father, and He says it's essential for you too: "If you keep My commandments, you will abide in My love, just

as I have kept My Father's commandments and abide in His love"
(John 15:10).

Choosing to deal with sin means choosing obedience. Abiding
in Christ requires keeping short records with God. When you sin,
make sure you confess it right away, being assured that God "is faithful and just to forgive us our sins and to cleanse us from all unrigh-
teousness" (1 John1:9). Once you have dealt with your sin, you will
once again be walking in the Spirit.

You Can Do It, Dad!

I wish I was with you right now to give you a hearty pat on the
back. I know you are busy—what dad isn't? The very fact that you are
taking time out of your schedule to read a book about being a better
father says a lot about you and your heart.

God wants you to grow spiritually in Him—to grow as a husband, and to grow as a dad. We've discussed making choices, and
we've talked about how important it is for you as a father to walk by
the Spirit—to be a Spirit-filled man of God.

I thank God that you are on His path and moving forward. You
can do it, Dad, so don't get discouraged. All growth takes place one
day at a time. Just be a man and a dad after God's own heart today...
and then wake up tomorrow and every tomorrow and do it again...
and again.

Here's how to walk by the Spirit:

> One foot in front of the other
> One thought at a time
> One sentence at a time
> One response at a time
> One decision at a time
> One minute at a time
> One day at a time
> And when you fail, stop (it),
> admit it, confess it, apologize for it, and go on.
> Leave it behind. Learn from it, but leave it.[3]

Small Steps That Make a Big Difference

1. *Seek a mentor.* A mentor can help you with your walk with God, your spiritual growth, and your role as a parent. Having a mentor is like having a personal trainer or coach who can assist you with your spiritual training. Pray and ask God to help you find someone who exhibits the spiritual maturity you desire for your own life. I know from experience what a great help a mentor can be. It's like the proverb says, "Iron sharpens iron, so one man sharpens another" (Proverbs 27:17 NASB).

2. *Join a men's group.* A men's Bible study or accountability group may be the place where you find a mentor as you observe the different men in the group. If the men are studying from a book, make sure you buy and commit to reading it and participating in the discussions. The more you are involved with other men who are pursuing spiritual growth, the more you will grow.

3. *Memorize Scripture.* Pick some important or favorite verses from the Bible and memorize them. And don't forget to have your children memorize them along with you. You'll be building some great memories while you learn God's Word together. The psalmist wrote, "Your word I have hidden in my heart, that I might not sin against you" (Psalm 119:11). Wherever you are and whatever is happening, you'll have God's Word right there in your mind and heart whenever trials or temptation come your way.

4. *Pray—and pray some more.* When you pray, you're acknowledging God as an active participant in your life. Taking time each day, as well as moment by moment throughout your day, will strengthen your spiritual life. This, in turn, will strengthen your marriage and the kind of influence you have on your children.

One father is more than a hundred schoolmasters.[4]
—GEORGE HERBERT

Teaching is a partnership with God.
You are not molding iron nor chiseling marble;
you are working with the Creator of the universe
in shaping human character and determining destiny.[1]

RUTH VAUGHAN

A Dad Who Is a Teacher

*These words which I command you today
shall be in your heart. You shall teach them
diligently to your children, and shall talk of them
when you sit in your house, when you walk by the way,
when you lie down, and when you rise up.*

DEUTERONOMY 6:6-7

March first!" Greg said to himself out loud. "Boy, I'll never forget this day, ever!" Then continuing to talk to himself, he said, "That's the day little Mary Lou was born!" Greg was talking as if March 1 had happened weeks ago, when in fact it was just yesterday! But a lot had happened, and it seemed like yesterday had happened long ago. Oh yes, life had changed. This was a whole new ball game!

After spending most of the day at the hospital, Greg had gone home and crawled into bed for a few hours of sleep. Then when he awoke, he got down on his knees for another session of prayer with God. As he had done the day before, he asked God for help as he tried his best to fulfill his new role as dad. Still not feeling all that confident about this awesome responsibility, and because it wasn't time to go back to the hospital yet, Greg decided to pick up his Bible to continue his daily reading schedule that he had started on January 1.

By this point Greg had gotten to Deuteronomy chapters 5–7. He was glad he had purchased a study Bible, for it helped to explain the passages he was reading. The backdrop of these chapters was that the children of Israel had been wandering in the wilderness for 40 years because they had failed to trust God to lead them into the Promised

Land. During the wanderings, an entire generation of people had died. So now Moses was addressing a new generation. He was preparing them both spiritually and physically for life in their new homeland. Greg hunched over his Bible on the kitchen table and began reading chapter 5, which was a review of God's Ten Commandments. Then he continued on to chapter 6. Upon reading verses 5-7, he suddenly sat up with amazement as he realized that God was giving him important guidance about how he should raise his little baby girl! He slowly read the verses again:

> You shall love the LORD your God with all your heart, with all your soul, and with all your strength. And these words which I command you today shall be in your heart. You shall teach them diligently to your children, and shall talk of them when you sit in your house, when you walk by the way, when you lie down, and when you rise up.

Back to the Basics

Every year, before the opening of baseball season, players go off to some warm-climate location for spring training. What's amazing is that it doesn't matter whether a player is a veteran with ten Golden Gloves and a huge contract, or a rookie called up from the minors. Every player begins camp on equal footing by focusing on the basics, like fielding and hitting. That's because the basics are important. Unless you master them, you won't do well.

Similarly, you and I as parents—and specifically as dads—need to periodically return to the basics, and remember the essential principles found in the Bible about how we are to raise our children.

When God spoke in Deuteronomy 6:5-7, that's exactly what He was doing with Moses and the Israelites. He was instructing them on the basics of parenting. And no matter how long you've been a dad, you can always use a refresher course in the basics of child-raising. Or maybe like Greg, you need to learn these principles for the first time. Whatever the case, let's take a closer look at Deuteronomy 6:5-7 and see what it says.

A Dad's First Assignment—Make God Your Priority

Who are you to love? We "love" a lot of things for a lot of different reasons. But God prescribes perimeters for your love. For example, He tells you what *not* to love: "Do not love the world or the things in the world" (1 John 2:15). And He tells you what you *are* to love and where that love is to be focused—"You shall love the LORD" (Deuteronomy 6:5). Because God commands it, you are expected to do this.

How focused is that love to be? The Lord goes a step farther and demands *all* your love. With every fiber of your being, every breath, every ounce of energy, every thought, every emotion and passion, every choice, God wants you to love Him—to think first of Him, to desire above all else to please Him. And that love is to be with all your heart, with all your soul, and with all your strength (see verse 5). As writer Matthew Henry summarizes, "He that is our all demands our all."[2]

Matthew Henry continues on to point out that your love for God is to be strong—it is to be lived out with great enthusiasm and fervency of affection. It is to be a love that burns like a sacred fire, a love that causes our every affection to flow toward Him.[3]

Love's Overflow

God wants you to obsess and focus on Him. How will this affect your love for your family? First, the more you love God, the more you will know about love. Next, the more you know about love, the more you will know about how to love. And finally, the more you know about how to love, the more you will love your wife and your children. When you love God as you should, your love will overflow to your family.

> When you love God as you should, your love will overflow to your family.

I like what C.S. Lewis wrote about his love for God and how it affected his relationship with his wife: "When I have learnt to love God better than my earthly dearest, I shall love my earthly dearest better than I do now."[4]

The Look of Love

What does that overflow love look like in real life? From the first moment you know a baby is on the way, all your thoughts, dreams, prayers, and goals should be focused toward that little one. You should be completely consumed with understanding what it means to be a dad, and specifically, a dad after God's own heart.

Your love for that anticipated child should start with helping your wife begin to prepare physically for the baby's arrival by making sure she takes care of her health. A healthy mom is more likely to have a healthy baby. It also usually means helping your wife by setting up some kind of nursery area for the new addition—a bassinet or crib, a blanket, a mobile, clothes, supplies, loads of diapers(!), maybe even painting or remodeling a room.

Then, as dad and leader of your growing family, your love looks to the financial needs of those in your home. This is a good time to sit down with your wife and discuss the future. If she's working, does she want or need to continue working? Maybe she can and wants to keep working for a while, or maybe she wants to quit. How can you make her dream a reality? Do you need to get a second job? Take on additional shifts? Work some overtime? In relation to your wife's job, what arrangements need to be made for her departure or leave of absence?

Are you beginning to see the extent of the sacrificial love that is necessary on your part as the preparations go on and on? This love makes it absolutely paramount that you, Dad, be part of these preparations. Love doesn't bail when the reality of a child begins to sink in. Love isn't being an absentee dad.

God's first assignment to every dad, then, is to love Him supremely. When you do, you will be much further down the road to being the kind of dad who, by God's grace, can raise children after His own heart. Because all of you—your heart, your soul, your mind, and your strength—is centered on God, your love will overflow to your family and your heart's desire will be to teach your children to love and follow Him too.

A Dad's Second Assignment—Internalize God's Word

What will it take to keep God's love uppermost in your heart and mind? In Deuteronomy 6, Moses is in the final weeks of his life. It has been 40 years since God's people left Egypt. They have endured 40 years of homeless wandering in the desert.

As Israel is camped on the banks of the Jordan River, a new generation was poised to proceed into the Promised Land. Moses restates the Law one more time to a new generation of Israelites before they move forward into the land. This new generation was born in the wilderness. They were all less than 40 years old, so any children they had would be young. As Moses speaks, he doesn't want them to merely hear the words of the Law and the Ten Commandments. No, he wants more—way more! He wants the words of the Law to go beyond their ears and reside in their hearts. "These words which I command you today shall be in your heart" (6:6).

God tells us in Deuteronomy 6:6 that His Word, the Bible, is to be in our hearts. What's in your heart? I don't know, but God tells you what's supposed to be there—His Word! He repeats this command several other places in the Bible:

> God encouraged Joshua, the new commander who would take Moses' place, "This Book of the Law shall not depart from your mouth, but you shall meditate in it day and night" (Joshua 1:8).

> The psalmist praised God that "Your word I have hidden in my heart, that I might not sin against you" (Psalm 119:11).

> An impassioned father urged his son to "keep my words, and treasure my commands within you…bind them on your fingers; write them on the tablet of your heart" (Proverbs 7:1-3).

> Zacharias, the father of John the Baptist, was definitely a dad after God's own heart. He is described as "righteous before God, walking in all the commandments and ordinances of the Lord blameless" (Luke 1:6). Paul said it this way: "Let the word of Christ dwell in you richly" (Colossians 3:16).

The message is repeated throughout the Bible, and it's loud, isn't it? God's Word is to be in your heart. He asks this of you and me as parents, as dads. Why? Because if truth resides in your heart, then you will have a source of guidance when you need help, strength, wisdom, and perseverance as a dad. And that's something you can pass on to your children.

Having and raising a child is perhaps the greatest earthly blessing you will ever enjoy. And, at the same time, it's the greatest challenge. But take heart—God's Word will always be there in you, with you, and for you as you teach your children in the ways of the Lord.

So God's second assignment for any and every dad is to be committed to His Word and to do whatever it takes to embed the teachings of Scripture in his heart and soul and mind. As I said earlier, you cannot impart what you do not possess. And this is the essence of Moses' instruction to parents. To teach and guide, lead and raise a child after God's own heart requires that God's truth be in your heart first. Only then will you possess something you can impart. And it's the most important thing you could ever pass on to your precious children—the truth about God and the salvation He extends through His Son, Jesus Christ.

Dad's Third Assignment—Teach God's Word

How do you help your children develop a heart for God's words? Deuteronomy 6:7 answers this question: "You shall teach them diligently to your children." We have been slowly working our way toward this important responsibility since we began the chapter, and by now you should have the motivation to do this. A dad who loves the Lord with all his heart and hides God's words in his heart will want to teach the Lord's truths to his sons and daughters.

Let's look more closely at the specific elements of Deuteronomy 6:7.

"You shall teach"

God says, "You shall teach…" A couple of the key ways to teach anything is by mouth and by model. In chapters 1 and 2 of this book, we saw how important it is to display a model of Christian character and conduct to our children.

As I write this, I am reminded of an evangelism seminar I conducted at UCLA. I posed a question to the group: "Who are the hardest students to reach with the gospel?" To my surprise, the consensus of the class was the children of nominal Sunday-only-Christian parents. The students of nominally "Christian" parents wanted nothing to do with a religion where the parents said one thing on Sundays and lived an entirely different life during the week.

This means you need to take your actions and attitudes around your children very seriously, especially if you claim to be a Christian. You need to be consistent. As the saying goes, "Don't just talk the talk, but make sure you walk the walk!"

As a dad, you teach by your life example. For some dads, this will be the most comfortable way to teach. Whether you find it comfortable or not, ultimately it means that you first need to have God's Word in your heart so you can consistently live it out before your children. God is not asking you to teach math or English. He is asking you to teach "these words which I command you" (verse 6).

Deuteronomy 6:7 tells dads (and let's not forget moms) to teach their children His Word, His ways, His truth. Now, God's Word is life-changing stuff! If you impart this wisdom to your children, it can help guide their lives and choices for as long as they live. This is truth that can pierce hearts and bring

> Teaching God's truth to your children...will shape their character and determine their destiny.

your children to Christ. Teaching God's truth to your children—as you are admonished to do in Deuteronomy 6:6-7—will shape their character and determine their destiny.

That's what happened to Timothy. When the apostle Paul wrote to his young trusted associate in ministry, he told Timothy "that from childhood you have known the Holy Scriptures, which are able to make you wise for salvation through faith which is in Christ Jesus" (2 Timothy 3:15).

God's Word is dynamite! Through the faithful obedience of a

mom and a grandmom who were faithful to teach little Timothy the sacred truths of Scripture, a way was paved for Timothy's salvation. Mom and Grandmom did their parts...and God certainly did His part!

So...shouldn't a dad after God's own heart—a dad who wants to raise children after God's own heart—take the teaching of Scripture seriously? If you are in this mind-set...

- Shouldn't you too be committed to instructing your children in God's ways?

- Shouldn't you plan to some extent how you will accomplish this goal?

- Shouldn't you schedule a time each day for some kind of formal time with them?

- Shouldn't you also encourage them to have some time alone with God in a quiet time?

- Shouldn't you coach them in ways to have daily devotions?

- Shouldn't you search for age-appropriate materials to complement your children's instruction?

- Shouldn't you be talking with other parents about how they live out God's instructions to teach their children biblical truth?

- Shouldn't you (and this is really important) pray daily about this job assignment from God, this teacher role He has personally given you as the leader of the family?

"Them diligently"

Next in Deuteronomy 6:7 God instructs you to "teach them diligently to your children." The "them" is God's Word and His commands. They are to be taught to your children. How much effort should you put into this? It should be done "diligently." And *diligent*, by the way, means being purposeful and conscientious in a task or duty.

Now give this some thought for a minute: What are you diligent about? Some dads are diligent about doing their jobs, which is a good thing because that is a biblical principle. Other dads are diligent about their sports and hobbies—or their car. Others are diligent about their health and they would never miss their daily run or exercise at the gym. On and on goes the list of ways in which men choose to be diligent instead of careless, lazy, or negligent.

Now switch your thoughts to being diligent when it comes to teaching spiritual truth to your children—versus leaving this all-important assignment to someone else, like your wife, a church leader, a Christian school, or a grandparent. Don't get me wrong—these other people are incredible and much-needed resources. But they are to be your *partners* in imparting truth, not your stand-ins or substitutes. You, as your children's father, are to be the primary teacher of truth to your children.

"You shall...talk of them"

Earlier we talked about the two ways we can give instruction—through our words, and through our example. The other way is through our everyday talk. This simply means making God's teachings a part of our everyday conversation.

This isn't as hard as we might think. And we shouldn't feel nervous about it just because we don't have a degree in education. That's not what God expects of parents. Rather, when it comes to teaching His truths to your children, He says, "You shall...talk of them when you sit in your house, when you walk by the way, when you lie down, and when you rise up" (verse 7).

No matter what your level of education, or whether you have any experience teaching—or how busy you are!—God expects you to pour His Word out of your heart and into your children's hearts. All this requires of you is...

> *Step #1*—Love the Lord with all your heart;
> *Step #2*—have God's Word in your heart; and then
> *Step #3*—teach His truths diligently by...talking.

"That's all there is to it?" you say. Yes, that's it—by talking.

"When you sit in your house"

Note where all your father-to-child talking and teaching is to take place—at home. Nothing could be easier or more natural or more convenient! You don't need elaborate lesson and activity plans. You don't need to dress up or create a special setting. You don't need to get into the car, go somewhere, or spend any money.

No. God simply says that "when you sit in your house," you are to talk about the Lord. That isn't very difficult, is it? You sit to relax. You sit to eat. You sit to visit. You sit to read. You sit to work on a puzzle or project or do homework together. And even outside the house, you sit whenever you are in the car together. That makes these low-key, sitting instances prime opportunities to talk about the Lord and His love and His promises. Of course, talking about God with your children can't take place with the distraction of the TV or video games. This means you are going to have to plan or designate times when these are turned off.

God continues on in Deuteronomy 6:7 and adds this to your talking times: "when you lie down, and when you rise up." Well, by now you know what you're supposed to do—talk about the Lord! You can help even your littlest children start and end their days with thoughts of God in their minds. Before you leave for work, you can go into your child's room and say, "This is the day the LORD has made; we will rejoice and be glad in it" (Psalm 118:24). Then you can add, "Rise and shine!"

Or you can call out to your daughter, "There you are, my precious blessing from God!" Or to your young guy, "How's God's little soldier today?" Then during the day, call your wife and ask her to put one or more of the children on the phone so you can share a Bible verse or just say how much you love and miss them.

And at night, prayer is the perfect way to put little—and big!—ones to bed. It puts their day and all that happened to rest. It calms any sorrows and soothes any hurts from the day. And it quells all fears. Like David articulated, "I lay down and slept; I awoke; for the LORD sustained me," and "I will both lie down in peace, and sleep; for you alone, O LORD, make me dwell in safety" (Psalms 3:5 and 4:8).

"When you walk by the way"

God not only says to talk to your children about Him at home; He also says you are to do the same outside the home—that is, "when you walk by the way." As your children get older, you'll want to schedule a "daddy outing" with each child weekly, if possible. A "date" with your girls, or some "guy time" are great opportunities to talk about the serious and the silly. This is walking by the way. These alone times with each child will allow you focused time to talk personally and privately with them, and especially about their relationship with God through Jesus Christ.

So God's third assignment to every dad is that he constantly be teaching and talking to his children about the Lord he loves. Teaching and talking. And talking and teaching. Home is the natural 24/7 place to impress God's truths upon your children. That's where they get to see and hear every day how important the Lord is to you and their mom. And beyond the home, as you "walk by the way," there are plenty of additional opportunities for you to tell your children about Him.

Make it a point to take advantage of the gift of such times. And if they are too few and far between, make them happen. As we learned earlier, you'll make time for what is truly important to you. So look at your schedule and figure out ways to carve out time together with your kids. Author Tedd Tripp challenges us with these words in his book *Shepherding a Child's Heart*:

> You shepherd your child in God's behalf. The task God has given you is not one that can be conveniently scheduled. It is a pervasive task. Training and shepherding are going on whenever you are with your children. Whether waking, walking, talking, or resting, you must be involved in helping your child to understand life, himself and his needs from a biblical perspective.[5]

You Can Do It, Dad

In my book *A Husband After God's Own Heart*[6] I shared the following story about the impact of a dad's informal teaching.

I was attending a seminar led by a special pastor and leader. As this man opened his talk, he shared that while he and his sister were growing up, his father spent a lot of time with them. The dad's policy was to spend an hour every evening after dinner with his children. Sometimes the hour was spent teaching from the Bible, or telling a Bible story. As the children got older, the father would talk to them about events in the newspaper and consider them in the light of biblical truth. These one-hour-a-day sessions lasted until the son left home to attend college.

What a great model of what we've been talking about in this chapter! If you want to be a dad after God's own heart and influence your children for God, you must have contact. And the impact you have upon them is in direct proportion to the time you spend with them—both formally and informally.

Small Steps That Make a Big Difference

1. *Take your role as a teacher seriously.* Teaching your children is your mandate. Think about it: The Christian faith is, humanly speaking, only one generation away from extinction. As I said earlier, that doesn't mean you have to teach "classroom style," but it does means you are to look for opportunities to continually impart God's truths to your children.

That's the responsibility God wanted to impress upon the Israelite parents—and by extension, to you. The parents and their faithful teaching about God were the hope for the next generation. If they didn't teach their children about God, then the following generation would have been godless. Make sure, Dad, that you are doing your part to instill the teachings of the Christian faith to your children. Then trust God to do His work in their hearts.

2. *Carve out time each day for your children.* Somehow you always manage to find the time to do what you think is important, right?

If spending time with your children is important to you, then you will make the time. You can't use the excuse, "I don't have time for special 'dad time' with my children" because there's always time—it's just a matter of how you are prioritizing it. It's great if Mom is spending time with the kids, but they need time with you as well. In fact, time spent with your family is usually the very best use of your time.

3. *Read God's Word and pass it on.* This brings us back to God's first step for dads: His Word must be in your heart. So be sure you are faithfully spending time in the Word and then sharing its truths and principles with your kids. See your children as your "Bible class" and even prepare for it. Choose something to study from the Bible or a book for kids. Take the kids on an outing to your local bookstore and look for materials for studying the Bible together with your children.

4. *Enlist your wife's help.* By that I don't mean pass the teaching off to your wife. Sure, she's probably with the children more than you are, but that doesn't negate your role and responsibility as a teacher. Work together as a team.

Tomorrow

I saw tomorrow marching by
on little children's feet
Within their forms and faces
read her prophecy complete.

I saw tomorrow look at me
from little children's eyes,
and I thought how carefully we'd teach,
if we were really wise![7]

Let no Christian parents fall into the delusion that Sunday school is intended to ease them of their personal duties. The first and most natural condition of things is for Christian parents to train up their own children in the nurture and admonition of the Lord.[1]

C.H. SPURGEON

4

A Dad Who Is a Trainer

Train up a child in the way he should go,
And when he is old he will not depart from it.

PROVERBS 22:6

Greg and Margaret were sitting together and holding hands as they listened to Bill, the teacher of their young marrieds' Sunday school class (as well as Greg's mentor). Bill was taking the couples through the book of Ephesians. He was a great teacher, and Greg felt honored that Bill had agreed to disciple him.

As Bill taught, Greg couldn't help but think, *There's no way I could ever get up and teach a class like this.* Just the thought of speaking in front of others made Greg's throat tight and dry. He imagined that being asked to teach would make him a candidate for the cardiac ward at the hospital where little Mary Lou has just been born.

Greg knew he wasn't a teacher, and that concerned him big time. That's because just a few weeks ago he had read Deuteronomy 6:7, which says, "You [dads] shall teach [the words of God] diligently to your children." At first when he read those words he had been excited at the thought of sharing Bible verses with little Mary Lou while she nestled on his lap as a toddler...and then later while she was a young girl, and still later as a teen.

But when he realized this meant being a teacher, he got nervous. In fact, a sick feeling came upon him every time he heard the word teach. It's true that Mary Lou was only six weeks old and there was plenty of time for Greg to prepare for this new role. But still...*teach* her? He wasn't sure he would be able to do that.

Greg made a mental note to himself to talk to Bill about his unsettled feeling during their next discipleship session.

Teaching Versus Training

Are you wondering what the difference is between teaching and training? Greg was convinced that he wasn't cut out to teach, but during their next discipleship meeting, Bill wouldn't let him off the hook. Bill explained to Greg that dads still need to communicate God's truths to their children, even if they don't feel like they're good teachers. Then Bill went on to share with Greg the difference between teaching and training.

Both teaching and training are important aspects of imparting information to others, but each aspect has its subtle differences. Follow along and visualize how each type of education—teaching and training—could and should be used to develop your children.

- —*Teaching* is mostly done in a classroom, while *training* is often done in the lab or workshop or on the job.

- —*Teaching* tends to emphasize theory, while *training* usually involves the practical.

- —*Teaching* generally provides the knowledge, while *training* helps apply that knowledge.

- —*Teaching* talks of tools and techniques, while *training* puts the tools and techniques into practice.

- —*Teaching* fills the mind, while *training* shapes habits.

- —*Teaching* usually has more immediate value, while *training* tends to offer more long-term value.

- —*Teaching* usually deals with general information, while *training* looks more closely at the specifics.

Benjamin Franklin summed up the differences between teaching and training this way. I added the words inside the brackets to help provide clarity:

Tell me and I forget.
Teach me and I remember.
Involve me [train me] and I learn.[2]

Training as Seen in the Book of Proverbs

Ever the wise mentor, Bill was ready for Greg's questions about teaching his children Christian truths. Bill explained, "The book of Proverbs can be a little confusing with its many statements dealing with different topics. It helps to see Proverbs more as a training manual than a teaching syllabus. Basically, God gave King Solomon and others the wisdom to write the book of Proverbs to give His people a training guide for wise living. If you and I were to be consistent about applying the practical admonitions found in Proverbs, we would experience a lot of spiritual growth."

Bill then went on to say, "Take Proverbs 22:6, for example. This is perhaps the best-known verse in Proverbs on child training." What Bill was sharing was aimed at Greg's concerns about the whole business of "teaching" the Bible to his little one. Bill continued, "Proverbs 22:6 states a concept: Give a child the direction for the way he should go. This implies that you as a parent, a dad, have a responsibility to your daughter and any other children you and Margaret have."

This definitely wasn't what Greg had wanted to hear. He was hoping to somehow be excused from having to teach.

Later that evening at home, as Greg reviewed his meeting notes and reflected on what Bill had said, he could still hear—in his mind—Bill's voice as he explained Proverbs 22:6: "Children are to be trained. It is assumed that the word 'you' is implied or understood in this verse. You should train up your children. And, from a biblical and historical perspective, the father has always been the trainer or has overseen the teaching of the children in the family. But this doesn't mean others can't be involved, like mothers and Sunday school teachers. So, yes, you are to train your children, to show them how to live the Christian life. But there's no need to view this responsibility as a one-man show. God has given fathers plenty of resources to help in the training process."

We've seen the subtle differences between teaching and training as it applies to present-day practices, but in the original Hebrew text of Proverbs 22:6, the word means "to dedicate," as in dedicating a house. A dedicated house was set aside for a particular use for a particular family. It could also include the idea of narrowing, or hedging in. You could say that according to these different Hebrew meanings of the word "train," you and others who teach alongside you are working to narrow your child's conduct toward a certain direction. And what direction is that? You want to direct your child away from evil and toward godliness—"in the way he should go."

Next comes the result: "And when he is old he will not depart from it." What does "it" refer to? The direction toward God—toward wisdom. These two destinations are tied together as stated in Proverbs 9:10: "The fear of the LORD is the beginning of wisdom."

You as a parent are to be actively training your children every day to love God and walk in His wisdom. It's an established fact that early training normally results in lifelong habits. Therefore, it's never too early to start. And I would emphasize it's never too late either.

Many parents often become confused and bitter when their children grow up and seem to veer away from the way they were trained. But remember your role: You as a parent are instructed and expected to faithfully teach and train your children in God's Word and to direct them toward God's wisdom. You do this with teaching and with consistent, loving discipline throughout the child's time in the home. And when your children leave home, then you must place them on the altar of God's grace.

Training Ground—The Church

Greg continued to reflect on what Bill had told him. At one point, Bill had paused momentarily and said, "Greg, are you feeling a bit overwhelmed with what God is asking of you as a dad? Actually, in a sense, you should be blown away by the task that's been given to you. But, as I'll keep reminding you, God has given you lots of backup for the training process for your children."

Bill had then pointed out that the family home was one of two important places where both teaching and training are to take place. "The home is the logical and natural place for children to gain wisdom. And the other important place is your church."

"If church is so important," Greg asked, "why do parents, and especially dads, treat going to church as optional?" Bill had heard this question before and asked it often himself. He commented, "It's amazing how many excuses people can come up with for not wanting to do something, isn't it? Unfortunately, dads lead the way in making excuses about how the family spends Sundays."

Here are a few of the excuses dads will give for not going to church:

Excuse #1—"Church isn't all that important."

Some dads see church attendance as optional. They don't appreciate its significance in life, and especially in the spiritual development of their children. These same dads also don't see the importance of church for their own spiritual condition. This gets back to their spiritual temperature. If Dad sees the church as an important place for his own spiritual training, he will want that for his family too.

Some dads may see a church as merely a place to hang out on Sunday if you have nothing else to do, or a place to go when the weather is too wet or cold to play golf or go camping.

But a church isn't a place or a building. A church is made up of people the apostle Peter describes as "living stones, [who] are being built up a spiritual house, a holy priesthood, to offer up spiritual sacrifices acceptable to God through Jesus Christ" (1 Peter 2:5).

Excuse #2—"Sunday is the only day we have to be together as a family at home."

It's true that Sunday provides an opportunity for the family to relax at home without the pressures of jobs and school. But if it's important, then it should be worth the time and effort. It is for my son-in-law, Paul, who is an XO (Executive Officer, second in command) of a nuclear submarine. Paul leaves his home at 5:00 am and doesn't get home many nights until 8:00 or 9:00 pm. Yet on the one day he is free from his grueling, 16-hour days six days a week, he has his family at church, starting with two teens who must be at the church at 6:30 am to rehearse with the worship team.

> **If Dad sees the church as an important place for his own spiritual training, he will want that for his family too.**

If you want Christ to be the foundation for your family, church needs to be a priority. Let Christ provide the church as the glue that holds your family together. Don't deprive your children of interacting with other Christians and of participating in the ministry of Christ's Spirit through gifted preachers, teachers, and youth leaders. Set aside time in the morning with God's people. You still have the rest of the day to spend time with your family.

Excuse #3—"I work on Sundays."

Maybe there's nothing you can do about your work schedule. But sometimes people are able to talk with their boss and work out an arrangement that allows them to still go to church in the morning and make up their work later that day or some other day. Give it a try. Ask to switch days with someone so you can have Sundays off, and see what happens. And if you can't get off Sunday morning, many churches have a Sunday evening service or even a weeknight service that offers classes and activities for the children.

Excuse #4—"Sunday is when our kids have their soccer games."

The danger of this excuse is that it communicates that a game like soccer or baseball or basketball is more important than learning about Jesus and growing spiritually. When you sign up your kids for a sport or activity, check to see if it's going to prevent you from going to church as a family. This kind of decision is a serious choice that, ultimately, can have eternal consequences. Hear what Jesus says about His concern for children: "Let the little children come to Me, and do not forbid them; for of such is the kingdom of heaven" (Matthew 19:14).

Jesus is concerned for the spiritual welfare of your children, even if you aren't. Yes, there are certain benefits that sports can offer to your children. But the far greater benefits—the lifelong and eternal ones—will be found at church. So make an effort to get involved in sports activites that won't require you to sacrifice going to church, where your children can learn about God's love and His desire for their salvation.

Excuse #5—"My kids don't like the youth group. They don't feel like they belong."

This excuse is a little like catering to a child who doesn't like medicine. Do you say to your child, "Well, that's okay—you don't have to take the medicine even though it will help you get well." Sounds pretty silly, doesn't it? Don't let your children come up with an excuse for not going to church or getting involved with other kids at church. Challenge them to give the youth group a chance. Go to their class yourself as an observer. Join the group as one of the adult helpers. Encourage your kids to bring a friend or two. Do whatever it takes to make youth group happen.

Excuse #6—"We're afraid our little ones will catch an illness from the other kids."

Usually this is more of a mother's concern. But if it comes up, keep in mind that most churches today are very serious about caring for children's health by carefully sanitizing the nurseries and children's classrooms. You can ask what your church is doing. You can also volunteer to be one of the persons who does the sanitizing. And if you're still not sure, perhaps you can take your children into the worship service with you, or sit in the "cry room" if your church has one. Do what you can, and don't forget to trust your children's care and health in the hands of their loving heavenly Father.

Excuse #7—"My children go to a Christian school. They get everything they need there."

The rationale in this case is parents are concerned about their little darlings being exposed to religion 24/7. They think their children need a break from "too much church stuff." It's true Christian schools provide a wonderful, safe atmosphere that generally centers around religious beliefs. But attendance at Christian schools is not commanded in the Bible, whereas church attendance is. We are told to "consider one another in order to stir up love and good works, not forsaking the assembling of ourselves together, as is the manner of some, but exhorting one another" (Hebrews 10:24-25).

Also, the function of a Christian school is different from that of a church. At the school, your children are receiving an education. But at church, they are worshipping God, learning from His Word, and being spiritually encouraged by other Christian adults and kids.

Why Is Church Important?

After Bill explained the various excuses to Greg, he then shared why church is such a vital training ground for a family's spiritual life. He gave five reasons:

Reason #1—Church is a place where you go to learn about what's truly important in life. And every time you go there, you are communicating that you value what church has to offer. If you are lax, haphazard, and inconsistent in your church attendance, this will speak volumes to your children. If church isn't that important to you, then why should it be important to them?

Reason #2—Church is a place where your family hears the preaching and teaching of God's Word. God has given gifted men to the church to communicate the truths of Scripture to the people. A pastor's messages and a teacher's instruction can help you and your family to grow in your understanding of the Bible.

Reason #3—Church is a place where like-minded people can join together in unified worship (1 Timothy 2:8-12). Worship is more than uttering a prayer around a fire on a family camping trip that's used as a substitute for church worship. Worship with others strengthens you as you step out of the world for a time and spend that time focusing on God with fellow believers. You and your family need this weekly exposure to unified worship and fellowship, for it strengthens and encourages you spiritually.

Reason #4—Church is a place where you, your wife, and your children have the opportunity to serve others. As a Christian, you are given spiritual abilities (1 Corinthians 12:7) that are to be used to build up other members of the church, the body of Christ. As your children see you serving others, they will begin to understand the importance of ministry and want to do the same.

Reason #5—Church is a place where your children can meet and become friends with other Christian kids and young people. Their friendships with believers will strengthen and sustain your kids when they are exposed to a world of unbelief outside the church, They will realize that it's not just Mom and Dad who are committed to Christ, but also kids their own age.

You Can Do It, Dad!

I've been reading a book about "Easy" Company, a part of the 506th Parachute Infantry Regiment of the 101st Airborne Division. The book is titled *Band of Brothers*, and it was written by Stephen E. Ambrose. The idea for creating an elite fighting group like the Army Rangers or Navy SEALs did not exist before World War II. But as senior military leaders began to plan for the invasion of Europe, they came up with the concept for these groups. They were called Airborne units. These units were comprised of raw recruits who volunteered to come together for a special purpose, and ultimately, they became among the finest groups of warriors America had ever fielded.

What made this group of men, this band of brothers, so effective? On one word—training. From the time of their induction until they were dropped behind enemy lines in France on D-Day minus one, they had spent almost every day for months preparing for that one drop.

What does this have to do with you and your children? I think you know the answer. The commanders who formed the 506th Parachute Infantry Regiment knew what was needed to fight and survive, so they gave these men the training they needed to prepare them for the battles to come.

You, like those Airborne commanders, know what your children are facing and must deal with outside your home. You also know that without the proper training and preparation, your children are in danger and at risk. It's up to you, as their father, to do whatever you can do to prepare them for the battles they will face.

This chapter has been about the importance of your church as a basic training ground for your children. Team up with your church—a resource from God—to give your children wisdom for dealing with life's battles and spiritual warfare.

Small Steps That Make a Big Difference

1. *Make going to church a priority in your life.* Start by seeing church as a unique, special place where you go to worship with other believers. A place where you are taught God's Word. A place where you can mature spiritually and serve others.

2. *Make going to church a priority for your family.* If church is a priority for you, then your family will follow your leadership. If you're excited about church, they will be too.

3. *Make sure you talk about church.* You talk about what's important to you. If all week you are talking about church and your excitement, then the family will get excited too. Take notes during your pastor's sermon and go over those notes with your wife and kids during Sunday dinner.

4. *Make sure you and your family are as involved at church as is reasonable.* Attend the Saturday men's group. Encourage your wife to join a women's Bible study. Do whatever it takes to get your kids to their youth groups and activities and camps.

The best way to train up a child the way he should go,
is to travel that road occasionally yourself.

—Author unknown

The secret of discipline is motivation.
When a man is sufficiently motivated,
discipline will take care of itself.[1]

—SIR ALEXANDER PATERSON

5

A Dad Who Is an Instructor

To obey is better than sacrifice.

1 SAMUEL 15:22

The plan for Greg's discipleship meeting with Bill this week was for them to go over the basics of the Christian faith. Greg agreed with Bill that a good foundation for anything started with the basics— one plus one, ABC, those sorts of things. When the meeting started, Greg couldn't help immediately thinking of his days in Army basic training. "Bill," Greg asked, "do you remember the name of your drill sergeant at Marine boot camp?"

"Oh, yeah. Are you kidding? I could never forget him!" Bill exclaimed. "He was Gunnery Sergeant Bob Osterman. Boy, was he tough on us! He pushed, prodded, and led my training platoon through three months of absolute torture. But in the end, we were the best platoon out of that training cycle. We scored highest in physical fitness and had the highest scores on the rifle range. He definitely prepared us for what we faced in Afghanistan."

Greg then shared with Bill his own set of memories of his drill sergeant. Then they laughed as they argued over which branch of the military was the best and which one of them had the toughest drill instructor.

Taking on Another Mission

Today we come to a new task in your mission of being a dad after God's own heart. We are adding the role of "drill sergeant"— or instructor. Like Greg and Bill, I have similar memories of my instructor in basic training. Those who are chosen to become drill sergeants are given that task because they are serious, well-seasoned, and battle hardened. Their job is to take a raw recruit and make him into a soldier in only a few months. The tougher they are on the recruits on the training ground, the more likely a soldier will survive on the battlefield.

Now, maybe you are thinking that in the military, drill sergeants aren't always nice people. But they aren't out to win a popularity contest. Their job is to train for survival in battle. As we look to their example, be aware that I am *not* asking you to emulate their harshness. Rather, I am encouraging you to emulate their tenacity toward preparing soldiers—in your case, your children—for survival on the battlefield of life.

As a dad, one of your jobs is to take a raw recruit—your child—and turn him or her into a godly man or godly woman who will love Jesus and, in turn, train up yet another generation to follow the Lord.

Also, whereas a drill sergeant has a recruit for only two or three months, you have your children for about 20 years! And you get to train and instruct them every day. Because God gives you many years to raise up your children, you have many opportunities to influence and train them up—in every area of life! So welcome to God's rank of drill sergeants.

What is the objective of your time spent instructing and training your children? It is first and foremost to help them develop a heart that follows God, that delights in being responsive to Him and His commands. Your goal is to nurture in them a heart that obeys.

You know all too well that even from an early age, the human spirit wants to rebel against authority—especially God's authority. As the joke goes, "My child's first word was *no*." So don't take it personally when your little ones say no—even dozens of times a day.

Your challenge is to patiently but firmly train your children's hearts to want to obey different types of authority. Obeying God is first on the list. Obeying their parents comes next, then teachers at school, and rules and laws in general follow right behind.

Two Kinds of Hearts

If you've read any of my books with *After God's Own Heart*[2] in the title, you know this phrase comes from Acts 13:22, where God gave this testimony about the man David: "I have found David the son of Jesse, a man after My own heart, who will do all My will." This commentary was in sharp contrast to the character of Saul, who was the reigning king of Israel. These two men had two different kinds of hearts.

David had an obedient heart. In time, and after help from God, David always responded to the Lord God with an obedient heart to do what was right (see 2 Samuel 12:13; 24:10). He yearned to follow God and do His will. He said, "Create in me a clean heart, O God, and renew a steadfast spirit within me" (Psalm 51:10).

Saul, however, had a selfish heart. He wasn't concerned about following God's will. He only wanted to do things his way. This became apparent when he didn't carry out the exact instructions God had given about destroying all the Amalekites and their belongings. The command was firm, and allowed for no exceptions. Instead, Saul spared the Amalekite king, Agag, and let the Israelites take the choice spoils from their victory over the Amalekites, including "the best of the sheep, the oxen, the fatlings, the lambs" (1 Samuel 15:9). When Samuel arrived on the scene, Saul claimed he had followed God's instructions. But Samuel could hear the sheep and oxen that had been taken from the Amalekites, and asked Saul, "What then is this...which I hear?" (verse 14). Saul tried to justify and excuse his disobedience, but the true nature of his heart had already been revealed. God wasn't interested in his excuses. Here's what Samuel said God desired:

> Has the LORD as great delight in burnt offerings and
> sacrifices, as in obeying the voice of the LORD? Behold,
> to obey is better than sacrifice, and to heed than the
> fat of rams. For rebellion is as the sin of witchcraft,
> and stubbornness is as iniquity and idolatry. Because
> you have rejected the word of the LORD, He also has
> rejected you from being king (1 Samuel 15:22-23).

God gave both Saul and David the same opportunity—to lead the nation of Israel. But in the end, they walked two different paths. David walked toward God, and Saul walked away from God.

Successful Training Starts with You

Hopefully you are continuing to concentrate on your first mission assignment as a dad who wants to raise children after God's own heart. Mission #1 is to be training yourself. My drill sergeant didn't ask anything of me that he hadn't already done himself and wasn't willing to do again. In fact, even though he was probably 30 years older than all of us recruits, he did everything better than we did!

Your children need you to model a love for God and a desire to follow His will. Where else are they going to see godly character up close and personal and daily, if not in you? So a major step in helping your children to develop a heart of obedience is letting them see obedience lived out in you. This is your passive instruction—teaching by your example.

God knows we need to know our limits and boundaries. That's why He gave us His Word. Obviously the Bible sets the ultimate standards for our conduct: "All Scripture is given by inspiration of God, and is profitable for doctrine, for reproof, for correction, for instruction in righteousness" (2 Timothy 3:16). That's why raising children after God's own heart starts with your heart of obedience. How can a child learn obedience from a disobedient father? It's not possible. An obedient child learns from the example of an obedient dad—a dad who follows God's Word.

> An obedient child learns from the example of an obedient dad—a dad who follows God's Word.

Areas That Require Discipline

I know the concept of discipline isn't very socially acceptable today. And it's true that part of this concern is justified because there is so much child abuse. But we are talking about a discipline based on *love* for a child and a *respect* for God's pattern of dealing with us. God's model is not based on anger or evil intent. Here's what God says about discipline, beginning with Proverbs 3:11-12:

> My son, do not despise the chastening of the LORD,
> Nor detest His correction;

For whom the LORD loves He corrects,
Just as a father the son in whom he delights.

The writer of Hebrews also discusses the discipline of the Lord:

> You have forgotten the exhortation which speaks to
> you as to sons: "My son, do not despise the chasten-
> ing of the LORD, nor be discouraged when you are
> rebuked by Him; for whom the LORD loves He chas-
> tens, and scourges every son whom He receives." If you
> endure chastening, God deals with you as with sons;
> for what son is there whom a father does not chasten?
> (Hebrews 12:5-7).

What does discipline produce? The writer of Hebrews gives this answer: "Now no chastening seems to be joyful for the present, but painful; nevertheless, afterward it yields the peaceable fruit of righteousness to those who have been trained by it" (Hebrews 12:11).

God is asking you, as a dad, as a godly drill instructor, to discipline your children with loving caution, as seen in these two verses:

> Do not provoke your children to wrath (Ephesians 6:4).

> Fathers, do not provoke your children, lest they
> become discouraged (Colossians 3:21).

In both of the verses above, fathers are warned by the apostle Paul not to make unreasonable demands or inflict harsh discipline that might drive their children to anger, despair, and resentment. This won't happen when a dad is walking by the Spirit and exhibiting love and self-control.

Now, where is the best place to instruct your children?

A Boot Camp Called *Home*

Your home becomes a perfect "training facility" for preparing your children to become a godly man or woman. And to make the training easy, God has given one specific command for you to teach your children: "Honor your father and mother" (Ephesians 6:2). That's it!

And that's why obedience starts at home. If your children learn this one command, then they are each well on their way to becoming not only a child after God's own heart, but someday, a man or woman after God's own heart.

Does this verse sound a little self-serving to you? Perhaps so. But God knows that if your children can learn obedience at home to you and their mother, then they will be more responsive to being obedient and submissive to God, to His Word, to the laws of the land, and to authorities at school and in society.

Obedience in Action

Your children have one command—"honor"—but they will need to be trained so as to see obedience as a key element of who they are as your child and a child of the King. And this is the hard part: You as a parent are commanded by God to discipline and correct your children so that they learn obedience. (I can't repeat myself enough, but with all the child abuse that's so prevalent these days, these biblical commands regarding discipline are not "politically correct." But if you are walking by God's Spirit, you will apply discipline in a proper and loving manner.)

Here's more of what God's Word has to say:

> He who spares his rod hates his son, but he who loves him disciplines him promptly (Proverbs 13:24).

> Chasten your son while there is hope, and do not set your heart on his destruction (Proverbs 19:18).

> Foolishness is bound up in the heart of a child; the rod of correction will drive it far from him (Proverbs 22:15).

> Do not withhold correction from a child, for if you beat him with a rod, he will not die. You shall beat him with a rod, and deliver his soul from hell (Proverbs 23:13-14).

> Correct your son, and he will give you rest; yes, he will give delight to your soul (Proverbs 29:17).

No sergeant would ever have a soldier in his unit who doesn't listen to him and do what he says immediately. In the same way, your children need to follow your rules. This is why God's Word says you are to apply discipline to the process.

But unfortunately, discipline is a difficult concept for many dads to grasp or apply, for a number of reasons. See if you can spot yourself in any of these reasons listed below. Which excuses apply to you? With that in mind, set a goal of making changes.

10 Reasons Dads Don't Discipline

1. I'm afraid of today's cultural stigma against discipline.

2. I can't bear to cause any pain. There are other ways to get through to a child.

3. It's enough to simply try to reason with a child. Therefore, there's no need for physical discipline. Give a child time, and sooner or later he or she will come around and respond positively.

4. Children are basically good and will grow out of their state of rebellion. Just give them time.

5. Discipline is barbaric and smacks of "Dark Age" thinking.

6. My wife and I don't agree on how to discipline, so we don't. I just hope things will turn out okay.

7. I don't know how to discipline. I'm afraid I'll do it wrong and damage my little ones' mental state.

8. Confrontation is not my thing. I'll let my wife and the teachers at school deal with my kids' behavioral issues.

9. I am not sure I agree with or understand what the Bible says about this matter of discipline.

10. I'm too busy to bother with the children. I'll let my wife deal with discipline issues. She does a better job anyway.

Establish Goals for Each Child

One of the first things the military does for all new recruits is establish training goals for them when they enter the service. The training goals or objectives are set, a schedule is made, and progress is noted. When Bill and Greg were enlisted, they had training goals set for them by their instructors. I had training goals set for me too. From the time I entered the Army until I retired as a Reserve Army Officer, I also made my own training objectives, and I also helped others set theirs. The Army was always looking for ways to motivate, monitor, and manage the progress of each soldier. What better way to motivate than to have you compete against your own goals?

So, unless you can think of a better model, why not take a page out of the military's training manual and create some achievable training objectives for each of your children? These goals are dynamic and will change as each child matures. You can't anticipate your children's future, but you can help prepare them to function well and provide for themselves.

You Can Do It, Dad!

God has given you the honor and privilege—and responsibility—of instructing each of your children. He's counting on you to do your job, to train them up in the way they should go. And your ultimate goal as an instructor is to nurture in your children a heart that wants to obey and please Jesus. A heart that desires to do God's will out of love for Him. A heart that seeks to please God even when you aren't around.

How is this done? Here are a couple of my favorite Bible verses for approaching tasks or assignments that look too daunting, too impossible:

> His divine power has given to us all things that pertain to life and godliness, through the knowledge of Him who called us by glory and virtue (2 Peter 1:3).

> I can do all things through Christ who strengthens me (Philippians 4:13).

You can do it, Dad. By God's grace, you can do it. You have God's Word. You have God's wisdom—when you ask for it and want it. You have older dads in the church who will gladly pass on their knowledge and experience. Team up with your wife and count on God's help. You can live out your role of instructing your children in the ways of the Lord.

Small Steps That Make a Big Difference

1. *Start with the basics.* It's never too early to start preparing your children for real life, and it's certainly never too late to begin training them in the basics. If you are starting when they are older, the challenges—and maybe even resistance—may be greater. But with your faithful persistence and a heart full of love, the blessings will be great too! In your prayer notebook or prayer list, write down your goals for each of your children.

2. *Enroll in a parenting class at church.* Maybe you're like I was, and you don't have a clue about being a Christian dad. So sign up for a parenting class. You'll learn biblical principles for raising children—principles that will stand the test of time and guide you in showing your children what God says about every practical area of their existence. And you can always read a parenting book. Read lots of books! Read something every day from a book just to keep you on your toes as you and your wife raise children from toddlers to teens. Don't miss out on the wisdom of the ages.

3. *Follow the godly example of others.* Think of a dad you admire. Then describe him. What is it you like about his parenting, or what is it you see that indicates he's a great parent? Look around at the parents you are acquainted with and pinpoint those who seem to have their act together. Start watching the way they deal with their children. Then do what my wife and I did. We had an issue with our girls during their teen years, so we went to four couples we had been observing and asked their advice. Their responses were encouraging, helpful, specific, and gave us direction. Many others have preceded you on the road of parenting. Watch, look, listen, and ask them questions.

And don't forget to write down and save what they say. More than that, put their advice to work!

4. *Keep adjusting.* Things change. You change. Your children change. The family makeup changes. Maybe you will move to a new state—or move often. Or someone's job changes. And, most of all, hopefully you are changing into a more Christlike man and dad. So plan to review and adjust your child-raising strategies regularly. Evaluate your training and methods of discipline frequently. What's working? What's not? Pray, and don't be afraid—or too proud—to seek advice if things aren't going the way you would like. And be willing to make adjustments. There's plenty of help out there, if you will just ask! What adjustments do you need to make today?

5. *Enjoy the ride.* Being a dad is a big job, a 24/7 occupation, but it can and should be fun too. Being an instructor takes time, effort, and planning, but that doesn't mean you and your children can't have fun in the process. Be sure and plan in lots of fun.

Make us masters of ourselves
that we may be the servants of others.[3]
Sir Alexander Paterson

I can exert no mighty influence
to make a place for you in men's affairs;
but lift to God in secret audience
unceasing prayers.[1]

MERRILL C. TENNEY

A Dad Who Is an Intercessor

Ask, and it will be given to you;
seek, and you will find;
knock, and it will be opened to you.
For everyone who asks receives,
and he who seeks finds,
and to him who knocks it will be opened.

MATTHEW 7:7-8

How could this be?" Greg mumbled to himself as he paced the hospital waiting room. Earlier this morning when he pulled out of the driveway, Margaret and little Mary Lou had waved good-bye to him with smiles on their faces. These last six months had been such a joy as he and Margaret had witnessed the growth and development of their first child. Greg's life had been wonderful since he married Margaret. With her strong Christian background, she had been such a blessing and source of strength. And now with little Mary Lou added to the family, life had been incredible. And then he had received an urgent phone call from the hospital.

Greg had been in a meeting at the office when he was asked to step out and take the call. That's when he found out Margaret and Mary Lou had been in a terrible car accident. Apparently a drunk driver had run a red light and broadsided Margaret's car. Both mother and daughter were in critical condition in the ICU.

Suddenly Greg felt like his life was crumbling apart. It seemed he was in danger of losing everything he held dear. His first reaction was to blame someone…anyone! He even wanted to blame God.

Why, God, would You allow this to happen to two such wonderful, inno-
cent people as Margaret and my little baby Mary Lou?

But then Greg dismissed these thoughts as he recalled his mentor's teaching about the nature of God. He could remember every
word Bill had said: "God's actions are always for our good and His
glory." Then Bill added, "We don't always understand, so ultimately
we must trust in God's goodness and grace." Those words came to
Greg's mind and helped to calm his heart.

So what would Bill do in a situation like this? Greg thought. Thinking back on their times together, he remembered that Bill often
reminded him that part of his role as a husband and dad was to pray
for his family—to intercede for the needs of his wife and child. At
that very moment, Greg dropped down on his knees while others
in the hospital waiting room looked on. With great intensity, Greg
began to intercede for the lives of his precious wife and his dear little girl.

Intercession Is a Vital Role for Dads

Most men are the do-it-yourself kind of guys. If it needs fixing,
they fix it themselves. (I'm giving you the benefit of the doubt on
this one. Maybe your wife has a different take on your willingness
to attempt to fix things yourself!) But normally, most men are or act
self-sufficient and have a hard time letting others help. For example,
they usually don't like to ask for directions.

As a result, many men—and maybe even you—have a hard time
depending upon God (including through prayer). This dependence
goes against all the "rules of masculinity." But to decline help—especially God's help—makes no sense. After all, men are also competitive and want to win. They want to be on the winning team.

So why not be on God's winning team? On this team, you have a
higher power—in fact, the highest power in the universe. You have
a team leader who possesses perfect wisdom and can give absolutely
100-percent correct guidance.

As a dad, you've likely discovered by now that being a father
requires more than you are capable of giving. This is exactly where
intercessory prayer comes in!

A Dad's Privilege

Most dads see providing for the physical needs of their families as a major duty, if not their primary one. The Bible speaks negatively about those who don't provide for their family when it says, "If anyone does not provide for his own, and especially for those of his household, he has denied the faith and is worse than an unbeliever" (1 Timothy 5:8).

The Bible also reveals that fathers are to provide not only for the physical needs of their children, but also for their spiritual needs. This is where intercessory prayer comes in. This kind of prayer petitions God with your concerns—not only for yourself, but also your family. The Bible has a few great examples of fathers who interceded for their children:

Job's intercession—The book of Job is considered by Bible scholars to be one of the oldest in the chronology of the Bible. Job lived about the same time as Abraham, and both men are viewed as great desert chiefs. As the spiritual and physical head of his family, Job saw his role as protector and mediator for his family.

Job not only provided for the physical well-being of his children, but he provided intercession for their spiritual well-being too. Notice this father's actions on behalf of his children: "Job...would rise early in the morning and offer burnt offerings according to the number of them all. For Job said, 'It may be that my sons have sinned and cursed God in their hearts'" (Job 1:5).

Job rose early in the morning, and his children were his first concern. He wasn't preoccupied with getting a head start on his work. Instead, he gave burnt offerings in case any of his sons had done something irreligious. What if any of them had "cursed God" in his heart? Job prayed and interceded quickly on behalf of his children. He did this regularly, and he made it his top priority.

Job's intercession wasn't a haphazard, slap-dash, once-in-a-greatwhile time of praying for his children. Rather, it was a constant, continual, and regular practice—one that he saw as a privilege.

Abraham's intercession—Maybe you've read or heard the Bible story about how Abraham offered Lot, his nephew, his choice of land for his herds. Lot looked at the desert, then turned and looked at a lush valley, and chose the valley for his cattle. The only problem was that, because of his choice, Lot and his family would have to live in close contact with the wicked people of Sodom and Gomorrah. At this point Abraham could have washed his hands of his foolish, greedy nephew. But that wasn't what happened.

In Genesis 18, God came to visit Abraham along with two of His angels on their way to destroy Sodom and Gomorrah. Abraham immediately began interceding for Lot and his family. He asked God, "Would you also destroy the righteous with the wicked?" (Genesis 18:23).

Abraham's intercession took on the form of bargaining on behalf of his nephew's family and any other righteous people who lived in those two cities. God agreed to spare Lot's family. Sadly, in the end, only Lot and his two daughters were spared alive (see Genesis 18:16-33; 19:23-30).

David's intercession—As a dad, you feel so helpless when your children get sick—especially when they come down with something serious. King David faced this reality. His infant son from his affair with another man's wife, Bathsheba, was gravely ill.

What was David's response as his child lay ill? "David therefore pleaded with God for the child, and David fasted and went in and lay all night on the ground" (2 Samuel 12:16). David interceded for his son's life for seven days, never ceasing until the child died (verse 18).

What was David's reaction to his baby son's death? He "arose from the ground, washed and anointed himself, and changed his clothes; and he went into the house of the LORD and worshiped" (verse 20). His sorrow had not lessened, but his role as intercessor for the child had ceased. After his child's death, he had to concentrate his attention on the rest of his family and on the nation (see verses 20-25).

Understanding Prayer

Scripture makes it clear that prayer plays a vital role in the life of a father who cares for his family. So if you want to be a better spiritual leader and a better dad, you'll want to make sure you have a good understanding of prayer.

That brings us to the all-important question: What exactly is prayer?

Prayer Is Communication

Prayer is talking to God. Communication is a two-way street. It requires active participation by both parties involved. In the case of God and His people, He communicates to us through His Word, and we respond to Him in prayer. This reveals one of the reasons we are often hesitant to pray: We don't know what to say to God because we haven't taken time to listen to Him in His Word.

Another reason we don't pray is because we are facing issues we aren't willing to deal with, such as areas of sin and disobedience we don't want to admit. Therefore we're reluctant to meet with God through His Word because we know it will point out the thoughts and intents of our heart (Hebrews 4:12).

When we let things get in the way of taking time to pray to God, it hurts our ability to be a good father. That's why it's so essential that we be willing to reach out and communicate with God, to talk to Him through prayer.

Prayer Is an Act of Faith

It's also important to recognize that prayer is an act of faith. You can't see God. Oh, you see His handiwork in creation (Romans 1:20), but God is Spirit. So when you pray, you are, in faith, asking an unseen God to hear and grant your request, to help you, to guide you. Therefore, prayer is the purest form of faith, which is "the substance of things hoped for, the evidence of things not seen" (Hebrews 11:1).

Yet at the same time, prayer is not based on imagination, and it isn't wishful thinking. It is founded on the promises of God—promises that are sure and will never change. For example, Jesus promised in John 16:24, "Until now you have asked nothing in My name. Ask, and you will receive, that your joy may be full."

God, by His very nature, is faithful and true. If He promises that

He hears and answers prayer, then believe what He says and pray with confidence.

Prayer Is a Privilege

Prayer is a privilege. Can you name the most important person you've ever had the privilege of meeting or talking with, even if it was for a brief moment or two? As a young boy, I touched the back of the hunting jacket worn by the great baseball centerfielder of the New York Yankees, Mickey Mantle. He was talking to the owner of a sporting goods store when I touched his jacket...and ran!

Yet amazingly, when we pray, we are talking with the God of the universe. And we don't need to be afraid! He encourages His people to come confidently before His throne to receive mercy and grace in times of need (Hebrews 4:16). What an honor He offers to us as Christians! He actually wants us to share our problems with Him. In our world full of people who are rushing around and too busy to stop, listen, and talk, it's reassuring to know that God is always available and ready to hear from us.

Prayer Expresses the Need and Submits to God's Will

Certainly at any minute of the day, your objective when you pray is the need that you are currently facing. Greg is a perfect example of a dad with an immediate need. His wife and child are in critical condition. He's not even sure they will live. His family's future is unknown and hanging by a thread.

Prayers of intercession should focus on knowing and accepting God's will. For example, when David's son was gravely ill, he prayed for the child to live. At the same time, David waited to know God's will on the matter. Once he knew God's will, he then needed to accept it.

Jesus is the ultimate and perfect example of a person who prayed regarding God's will and accepting it. Before His death, He prayed, "O My Father, if it is possible, let this cup pass from Me; nevertheless, not as I will, but as You will" (Matthew 26:39).

And He kept praying—three times. Why so many times? Jesus wasn't in conflict with the divine will. No, His conflict came as He wrestled in His humanity with what He knew He had to do—fulfill the Father's will and pay the price for sinners through His very painful death on the cross.

Prayer is your attempt to bring your will and desires in line with God's will. And God has provided you with two resources that can help you make sure you pray in harmony with His will.

First, the Holy Spirit. His ministry is to enlighten you in spiritual matters like prayer:

> Likewise the Spirit also helps in our weaknesses. For we do not know what we should pray for as we ought, but the Spirit Himself makes intercession for us with groanings which cannot be uttered. Now He who searches the hearts knows what the mind of the Spirit is, because He makes intercession for the saints according to the will of God (Romans 8:26-27).

Second, the Word of God also helps guide you and affirm God's will. The psalmist described how the Word directs you into the will of God: "Your word is a lamp to my feet and a light to my path" (Psalm 119:105).

As you...

> pray in faith (Matthew 21:22),
> pray without selfish motives (James 4:3), and
> pray according to the will of God (1 John 5:14-15),

you will be living the will of God while being led step by step, day by day, on the path to discovering God's will concerning your specific requests.

The Problem of Praying

With all of these assurances, resources, and promises, how come dads aren't more serious about praying? I have asked this myself and found some answers which I have written about in my book *The Man Who Makes a Difference.*[2] Here's what I said. Feel free to add to the list as you read along:

Worldliness—We live in the world, and there are very few voices urging God's people to pray. Prayer is a spiritual exercise. Therefore, we must work against the world and be men and dads of prayer. Yes we are *in* the world, but we are not to be *of* the world (John 17:16).

> **Prayer is your attempt to bring your will and desires in line with God's will.**

Busyness—We think we are so busy that we can't take time to stop and ask anything of God. Yet we are never too busy to play golf, go fishing or hunting, work on a hobby, or sit for three-plus hours watching our favorite sports team. We are never too busy to do the things that we think are important. Prayer doesn't seem to be that important, so it's no wonder it doesn't fit into a dad's "busy" schedule.

Faithlessness—For whatever reason, we doubt that things might actually have a different outcome because we prayed. But if we were confident and truly believed that God answers prayer, we wouldn't be able to wait to come into His presence with our needs and requests for our family. We'd be asking for God's help every minute—and enjoying His answers! James hit the nail on the head when he wrote, "You do not have because you do not ask" (James 4:2).

Distance—When we fail to talk to God, we feel like a stranger around Him. God never changes, moves, disappears, or loses interest in you. Dad, it's your job to close the gap. Take a simple step toward God and talk to Him. The more you talk to Him, the more comfortable you'll be as you communicate with Him. The more you communicate with Him, the more opportunities you'll have to pray for your family. And the more you ask of Him, the more answers and guidance you'll receive. Do these things, and you will no longer feel like a stranger around God.

Ignorance—We don't understand God's power and goodness. We don't grasp His desire and His ability to provide "far more abundantly beyond all that we ask or think" (Ephesians 3:20 NASB) and to "supply all of [our] need" (Philippians 4:19). If we did, we would pray more actively.

Sinfulness—We allow sin to build a barrier between us and our caring God. What did the psalmist say? "If I regard iniquity in my heart, the Lord will not hear" (Psalm 66:18). But when we confess our sin, the Lord's ears are open to our cries (Psalm 34:15).

Pridefulness—We, in essence, say to God, "I don't need You, God. I can take care of this one myself. I got this. No thanks!"

Think about this:

> The self-sufficient do not pray,
> the self-satisfied will not pray,
> the self-righteous cannot pray.[3]

For your family's sake, please don't ever be too proud to pray!

Inexperience—We don't pray; therefore, we don't know how to pray...so we don't pray! Prayer is like any skill—it becomes easier with repetition. The more we pray, the more we know how to pray. And the more we pray, the more answers to prayer we experience!

Laziness—This is probably the saddest excuse of all. We are just not willing to make the effort to pray, no matter how important it is... which, of course, affects our chances of having our prayers answered. Here's a prayer to pray: "Lord, may I never get to this place in my spiritual life!"

You Can Do It, Dad!

Did any of the reasons why men don't pray speak to you? (I know I got hit by one or two myself as I just read through this chapter again!) If you're like me, you know you aren't praying as you should. Hopefully you have identified some specific problem areas that are keeping you from being a praying dad who intercedes for his family. Here are some steps you can take to become a dad who is an intercessor.

Small Steps That Make a Big Difference

1. *Check out your excuses for not praying.* Identify the #1 culprit, and go from there. A problem defined is a problem half-solved. What will you do to eliminate this one problem, this one excuse, so you can get down to the business of praying for your children? You, Dad, are the head of your family, and your children are too important to allow anything—any excuse, any weakness, any sin—to keep you from your vital role as an intercessor for your family.

2. *Start a VIP prayer list.* At some time during the early part of your morning you probably put on your business hat and create a plan for your day. Maybe you make a list or use an app on your phone to put together a schedule, a to-do list, and note important details for the day. You should do the same when it comes to praying for your children. Be organized. List your prayer concerns, which are even more important than your business schedule. Use a section in your daily planner, or a notepad, or even a "prayer list" app on your phone to make a VIP prayer list with requests for each member of your family. Itemize the issues, decisions, projects, and problems that are affecting each person. Then, as a dad who is an intercessor, do some serious prayer business with God about the most important people in your life. Job was concerned for the spiritual condition of his children, and you need this same kind of oversight and care for the people in your life. Then, like an accountant, record the answers as they come in!

3. *Bolster your faith in answered prayer.* Don't be a dad who suffers from faithlessness. We described this kind of man as one who doubts that things might actually have a different outcome because he took time to pray. But if he were confident and truly believed that God answers prayer, he would be super-committed to the act of praying.

Bolster your faith by memorizing verses that speak of God's promises to answer prayer. Start with Matthew 7:7-8. Jesus told His disciples, "Ask, and it will be given to you; seek, and you will find; knock, and it will be opened to you. For everyone who asks receives, and he who seeks finds, and to him who knocks it will be opened."

It may help to remember the abbreviated version of this promise A-S-K:

> **A**sk…and you will receive.
> **S**eek…and you will find.
> **K**nock…and it will be opened.

If you've got a pen nearby, circle the word "will" in the verses above and again in the A-S-K acrostic. Yes, you can have faith in God's promise to answer your prayers.

4. *Start talking to God all day long*—Once again, prayer is just talking to God. You can't see Him, but He's there. So whether you're in your car, in the shower, jogging, or sitting at your computer, talk to God about your wife and children. Talk to Him about them all day long, wherever you are and whatever you are doing. He hears—and He responds. The Bible says "the eyes of the LORD are on the righteous, and His ears are open to their prayers" (1 Peter 3:12).

*The effective prayer of a righteous man
can accomplish much.*
JAMES 5:16 (NASB)

If any of you should ask me
for an epitome of the Christian religion,
I should say it is in that one word—prayer.[1]

C.H. Spurgeon

A Dad Who Is a Prayer Warrior

Put on the whole armor of God,
that you may be able to stand
against the wiles of the devil.

EPHESIANS 6:11

One month has crawled by since the car wreck that shook Greg's life, heart, and household. Margaret and little Mary Lou had been banged up pretty badly. There was no doubt about that! But God had been merciful, and Greg's two girls were making excellent progress in their recovery. The people at church had been incredible and had swooped in to take care of meals, provide nursing and child care, and help with any other needs that arose.

All through the month, Greg had continued to intercede for his family's recovery. God was graciously answering his prayers. Now as Greg and Bill sat across from each other at Bill's breakfast table, Bill began their meeting with a time of reminiscing—once again!—about their days of training to be soldiers. Bill, as a former Ranger, knew the most about training for battle, but Greg had his own skill set as well. After they shared a few "war stories," Bill asked Greg, "What was the military training us to be?" Greg thought for a minute, then said, "Warriors."

"That's right. And God has spent this past month taking you through another phase of training—prayer boot camp. Your learning to intercede for your family is preparing you to become a prayer warrior for your family. Intercession is *reactive*—responding to something that occurs and calls for intercession. But being a warrior is *proactive*—creating or controlling a situation rather than just responding to it." Bill then said, "So let's look at what's involved in becoming a prayer warrior."

What Does It Take to Be a Prayer Warrior?

In the last chapter, we learned some basics about prayer and interceding on behalf of your family. Intercession is a dad's responsibility and privilege. Who is more qualified than you, Dad, to be praying for your wife and kids? Commit yourself to praying regularly so you don't let them down in this key responsibility of a caring dad.

Now let's take the next step and look at your prayer life from a different perspective. Whereas intercession is more of a defensive tool, it's time for you to learn more about going on the offensive. Whether you know it or not, you are engaged in spiritual warfare not only for yourself, but also for your family. You are battling with the forces of evil for the spiritual well-being of your wife and children. God is asking you to lead and protect your family, and a key way to do that is to be a prayer warrior—God's "point man"—on the battlefield of life.

> God is asking you to lead and protect your family, and a key way to do that is to be a prayer warrior.

Just as a soldier is trained to fight a war, so you must be trained to fight and defend your family through prayer. God wants you to be prepared by not only knowing your enemy, but also defending your family from the enemy. The good news is that God has provided instructions that will ensure your victory. Ephesians 6:10-17 gives a detailed overview of what's necessary so you can fulfill your role as a prayer warrior.

Let's start with verses 10-13:

God's strength is your strength—"Be strong in the Lord and in the power of His might."

God's protection is assured—"Put on the whole armor of God, that you may be able to stand…"

Your enemy is clever—"…against the wiles of the devil."

Your battle is spiritual—"We do not wrestle against flesh and blood, but against principalities, against powers, against the rulers of the darkness of this age, against spiritual hosts of wickedness in the heavenly places."

Your protection is a choice—"Therefore take up the whole armor of God..."

Your endurance is assured—"...that you may be able to withstand in the evil day, and having done all, to stand."

What Does a Prayer Warrior Do?

What does a soldier do? Is he trained to run from the battle? No, he is prepared to stand his ground at all costs, even if it means giving up his own life. Continue reading verses 14-17 of Ephesians 6 and see how God's soldier responds to the threat of spiritual battle.

As you read, imagine a Roman soldier who is fully armed and ready to meet his enemy. Likewise, you are to prepare yourself for spiritual battle against the enemy of your family. Prayer is not just a nice little ritual you perform that gives you a warm, fuzzy feeling. And it's not something you do to check off a daily spiritual checklist. No, prayer is full-on warfare against the powers of darkness and evil. According to verses 14-17, you have the weapons needed for warfare—the waistband of truth, the breastplate of righteousness, the shoes of the gospel of peace, the shield of faith, and the helmet of salvation, which is the Word of God. After explaining how God has fully equipped you, the apostle Paul sums up your marching orders in verse 18 by defining how you are to carry out your mission of prayer.

The frequency of your prayers—"praying always." This is consistent with other verses that tell us to be "continuing steadfastly in prayer" (Romans 12:12), "continue earnestly in prayer" (Colossians 4:2), and "pray without ceasing" (1 Thessalonians 5:17).

The variety of your prayers—"with all prayer and supplication." Here, the word "prayer" refers to general requests, while "supplication" speaks of specific prayers. The apostle Paul is telling us that as prayer warriors, we are to be involved in all kinds of prayer as certain situations arise, whether in public or private. Nehemiah of the Old Testament is a prime example of a man who prayed fervently and regularly in his home (Nehemiah 1:4). But, when needed, he prayed a quick "arrow prayer" as I call it, while standing before the king (2:4).

The force of your prayers—"in the Spirit." Your power is not based on your own words, but in the force of God's will. To pray "in the Spirit" means you are praying for what is consistent with God's nature and will. When the Spirit is involved, He intercedes for you before God (Romans 8:26-27).

The attitude of your prayers—"being watchful to this end." The Lord Himself also voiced a similar concern when He told His disciples to "take heed, watch and pray" (Mark 13:33). Jesus sounded a warning to be on guard. The disciples were to stay awake and be alert, watch for approaching danger, and then through prayer, seek divine assistance. We are to do the same.

The resolve of your prayers—"with all perseverance and supplication." To illustrate the need for persistence in our prayers, Jesus gave the parable of the widow who repeatedly begged a judge for justice—until at last he finally gave in to her request. He finished by saying, "Shall God not avenge His own elect who cry out day and night to Him…?" (Luke 18:7).

The objects of your prayers—"for all the saints." The spiritual needs of your family and others in the family of God should be the focus of your prayers. That doesn't mean you don't pray for the lost. Rather, your primary focus is prayers "for all the saints," and in particular, your family. Here's a thought: You and your wife and perhaps some faithful grandparents may be the only people praying for your children. One of the greatest acts you can perform as a father is to pray regularly for your children.

What Is Required to Be a Prayer Warrior?

When my son-in-law called a Navy recruiter about becoming a Navy officer, he was given a set of requirements. He fulfilled those requirements and is now an executive officer on a nuclear submarine.

Just as a Navy officer must meet certain qualifications, there are some demanding requirements for being a prayer warrior. That's because spiritual warfare is serious business. How important is the spiritual well-being of your wife and children? And what are you willing to do—or to give up—so you can be an effective prayer warrior on behalf of your family? To be a tough fighter for the souls of your family requires two things of you right away.

Give Up Your Sin

First, give up your sin. By this I mean we dads must be willing to give up whatever does not please God, whatever goes against His Word and His will for us, whatever sin of any kind and any size.

Whether minuscule or massive on man's scale, in God's economy sin is sin...period. And sin interrupts your walk with God, your communication with Him, your fellowship with Him. God requires that you love and obey Him first, and then ask Him in prayer for what's important.

Maybe that's why prayer is so hard for you. You know God is holy, and you also know that you cannot simply rush to God and barge into His presence and ask Him for something when things aren't right in your walk with Him. You can't ask anything of a holy God unless you are a clean vessel. Before you pray for your wife and children, examine your own life, and make sure all is right with the Lord.

Throughout the Bible we see how crucial it is that we put away all sin, cleanse our hands and lives of sin, and purify our hearts (James 4:8). In short, God tells us not to pray until and unless we obey. The psalmist knew this. He wrote, "If I regard iniquity in my heart, the Lord will not hear" (Psalm 66:18). And Solomon put it this way: "One who turns away his ear from hearing the law, even his prayer is an abomination" (Proverbs 28:9). One scholar explained, "If we refuse to repent, if we harbor and cherish certain sins, then a wall is placed between us and God…Our attitude toward life should be one of confession and obedience."[2]

By contrast, if the desire of your heart is to follow God by tending to your walk with Him and turning away from sin, then He delights in listening to your prayers! The apostle Peter tells us, "The eyes of the LORD are on the righteous, and His ears are open to their prayers" (1 Peter 3:12).

Here's another challenging thought that hit home with me as a dad—and should do the same for you too! It was something my former pastor constantly reminded his congregation: "Put away your favorite sins. Greater things are at stake." Wow—greater things… like my children's salvation!

When we dads don't maintain our walk with the Lord, our family suffers. Why? Simply put—because we cannot pray effectively for them. Your sin causes you to be disqualified and ineffective as a prayer warrior. Sin silences your voice and voids your requests being lifted to God on your family's behalf and for their benefit. So God's message is for you to guard your walk with Him—to get rid of sin and get on your knees. Greater things are at stake!

Give Up Some Time

The second requirement for being an effective prayer warrior is to give up some time.

It's correct to say that anything that is truly important to you will require your time and attention. And praying for your wife and children is definitely a top priority. Think about it: Your children are your flesh and blood. They are closer to you than anyone else, other than your wife. That means you should be willing to give up some of the time you spend on *secondary* things so you have more time for the *primary* thing—praying for your wife and children.

Prayer requires time. And if your immediate response is that you're too busy to pray, then you need to somehow, somewhere, free up some time to carry out this priority. The Bible refers to this trade-off of lesser things for the greater things as "redeeming the time" (Ephesians 5:16). When it comes to you and your children, God has given you an allotted "season" of time with your children under your roof. It will truly fly by! That's why you must make the most of your time with them.

Here's a quick exercise I go through almost every day. Think about how much time you spend each day watching the news, or sports, or a favorite program or two, or even *The Weather Channel*. Or consider the amount of time you put into exercising, surfing the Internet, going on Facebook, or emailing friends and associates and taking care of your personal business. When you add up all this daily expenditure of your minutes and hours, you'll realize that you definitely have time for prayer—especially prayer for each child's life and soul. When you weigh how you spend so much of your time against how much time you spend praying for your children, the picture is shockingly clear.

I'm not saying there's necessarily anything wrong with spending time on daily activities. Of course you should stay on top of your finances, keep in touch with friends and business associates, help take care of others, inform yourself, and give yourself a boost through exercise or a coffee break. My point is this: If you think you don't have time to pray, then you need to look at your daily schedule and figure out how to adjust it so you can set aside time for one of the greatest, most rewarding activities of all—praying for your family.

Let's go another step further. As you prioritize your daily activities, put prayer first on the list. Make it your first order of business. A good life-management principle is to put any new discipline or activity first before any of your already-instilled practices. For example, let's say you jog every morning. That's a discipline that's already in place. So put prayer first—before you go jogging, which is already ingrained into your daily routine.

When you rearrange your schedule to reflect the priority of prayer, you will be blessed because when you pray, you are putting God first. You will benefit because you will change and grow as you talk to God. And blessing upon blessing, when you pray for your children, they will benefit as well. You will find yourself bonding tighter and tighter with your children as you invest your time in pouring out your heart and love for them to God.

So take time to pray. As Martin Luther said,

> The less I pray, the harder it gets;
> The more I pray, the better it goes.[3]

What Specifically Does a Prayer Warrior Do?

Earlier, we looked at Ephesians 6:18, which describes your responsibility as a prayer warrior. A part of that text says you are to pray "always with all prayer and supplication." The word for "prayer" in the original Greek text of the New Testament speaks of general prayer.

Often we pray in general terms like, "God, bless my family," or we pray for our nation. But the type of prayer warfare we are talking about for our family requires "pinpoint praying." That's what "supplication" means. Yes, it's okay for us to occasionally pray for "all the missionaries" and for "world peace," but your usual habit should be to focus in on specifics. And a key practical outcome of praying for specifics, you will know how God is answering your prayers.

> When you rearrange your schedule to reflect the priority of prayer, you will be blessed.

Praying for specifics is like "pinpoint bombing." This occurs when a laser beam "paints" the target for an incoming missile. Well, Dad, your prayers as a prayer warrior need to have this kind of precision. When you pray for your wife and children, it's good to be specific. Because this is a book on being a dad after God's heart, let's take a look at some specifics you should be praying for.

Pray for Your Child's Commitment to Christ

It should go without saying that a dad who loves the Lord with all his heart wants, above all else, for his children to belong to Christ—that they have a committed, vibrant love for Jesus. Therefore you, Dad, should focus all your parenting and praying on pointing them to God. The condition of each child's relationship with the Lord should be your first prayer each day. If you have a prayer notebook, this is the top item to write under each child's name. You can't give salvation to them—only God can do that. But you can intercede for them, asking for them to receive Christ. Or, if they are already a Christian, you can pray that they will pursue the Christian life wholeheartedly.

Pray for Your Child's Spiritual Growth

Beginning with the first chapter of this book, I have continually stressed the importance of the Bible in your spiritual growth. God has given you several remarkable gifts—His Son, salvation through His Son, and His Word. Jesus came to make salvation possible. Salvation through Jesus makes us children of God. And His Word is given to teach us and help us to know God and live His way, or according to His will.

When it comes to your children's spiritual growth, your prayers are vital. Like you, they need to be saved from their sins…which only a relationship with Jesus, God's Son, can accomplish. And they need to hear and know what the Bible teaches so that, by God's grace, they can live in obedience to God and avoid the kinds of mistakes many kids make while growing up.

So what can a dad do? And more specifically, what can *you* do? Pray and act! It's never too early to do this. If you've just found out your wife is expecting, then start praying. And from the day your child is born, read and verbalize God's Word to him or her. Again, it's never too early, as one faithful grandmother told me recently in a phone call.

This grandmother called to say that her daughter had been reading my wife's book *A Little Girl After God's Own Heart* [4] each night to her daughter when she was very little. Now, three years later, this girl is repeating verbatim the rhymes in that book, which are based on Galatians 5:22-23 to teach children the fruit of the Spirit. This grandmother related that one evening the entire family had gone out for dinner, and everyone at the table had received their food except the little girl. She told her family that she was being "patient" and rattled off from memory the eight-line rhyme for the fruit of the Spirit, patience. Even the things taught to very little children will be remembered as they grow up!

Commit yourself to doing what God tells parents to do—to talk to your children about the Lord from sunup to sundown (Deuteronomy 6:6-7). Whatever is in your heart is what will come out of your mouth. That's what Jesus said: "Out of the abundance of the heart [the] mouth speaks" (Luke 6:45). A dad's heart that feeds on God's Word daily is filled with thoughts of God and filled with God's thoughts. Then when he opens his mouth to speak to his children, out will come wisdom and truth about the thing that is most important to him—the Lord.

As time goes by and your children's lives move forward, keep praying with each new season of growth. Be ever the prayer warrior. And while you are praying, make it a goal to provide Christian resources for them at each learning level. For the very youngest, get an age-appropriate children's Bible with some key verses and illustrations in it to "read" while they are in their crib or car seat. Then as the children grow up, promote them to a simple picture Bible… to a more detailed children's Bible…a teen Bible…and then a study Bible. In this way you will help provide your children with an understanding of God's truth and fuel their growth as Christians.

Pray for Your Child's Physical Development

If you have boys, you can understand, relate to, and pray for their physical development at each stage in the growth process. But when it comes to daughters, you will want to work closely with your wife on praying with them. Having had only daughters, I learned early on that many of the issues important to them are different than the issues boys face.

My wife helped me to realize that struggles with peer pressure and self-image are a big deal for girls—and women too. Knowing this helped me to pray specifically for my girls. Your wife can help you to know how to best pray for your daughter. And when it comes to issues like self-image, both you and your wife can encourage your daughter to memorize Psalm 139:14: "I will praise You, for I am fearfully and wonderfully made; Marvelous are Your works, and that my soul knows very well."

As a dad, you are to be right there with your son or daughter in their trying times. You need to be God's go-to guy for your kids. If you are caring, loving, giving, and praying for them, then they will know that when they have a problem, they can come to you immediately. You will become someone they know they can trust, someone they can talk to and lean on.

Pray for Your Child's Mental Development

Your children's education will prepare them for life. Of course this starts at a very young age at home, and continues as your children go through school. Then there's the possibility of vocational training as well. In all of this, you want to be praying and stay involved with what is necessary for your children to learn.

All during this time, you should pray for your children's teachers, their aptitudes, their school friends, their extracurricular activities. There's a lot to pray for—tests, papers that need to be written, projects that need to be done, and placement exams. Be a praying dad with and for each child when it comes to their education and training. This requires your day-to-day involvement in their lives. Do your part by praying for your children's mental development.

You Can Do It, Dad!

Your job assignment as a dad is to recognize the need to be a prayer warrior. Prepare yourself for the battle. Know your enemy. And don't leave home without your spiritual armor. Dedicate your children to God, and dedicate yourself to praying for them. When you do this faithfully, you will be living out God's role for you as the spiritual leader of your family. You will be their prayer warrior. Be a dad like Job, who prayed for his many children every single day!

Small Steps That Make a Big Difference

1. *Check your armor.* My brother-in-law was trained as an Army Ranger, and part of his training was to parachute out of airplanes. He told me that before each jump, he would check the jump equipment of the man in front of him while, at the same time, his equipment was being checked by the man behind him. This extra attention to detail helped to ensure everyone's safety.

God is asking you to be a warrior, a prayer warrior for your children. Read again about what's involved when you "take up the whole armor of God" in Ephesians 6. Check yourself daily for God's armor.

And if you have a mentor, have him double-check you on it. The spiritual life of your family is at stake!

2. *Pray for wisdom.* Any smart dad (and I include you in this camp) knows that when it comes to doing what's right for his children, he needs help. That's why James 1:5 should be extremely reassuring: "If any of you lacks wisdom, let him ask of God, who gives to all liberally and without reproach, and it will be given to him."

So pray daily for wisdom from God about how to raise your children to know and love Him. Some aspects of God's will may be vague or hard to discern, but this part of God's will is absolutely clear: Your children are God's children, and you are God's appointed steward of their care. So don't mess up. Ask Him for His wisdom.

3. *Make a prayer sheet for each child.* If you don't have a prayer list for each member of your family, it won't be long before your prayers become too general and even rote, like "Dear God, please bless my kids today." Your children face unique issues each day and at each stage of their lives. Write out specific concerns for each child and go to war, praying like the Bible tells God's people to pray—always, frequently, fervently, constantly, continuously, in and about everything.

4. *Refuse to miss a day.* Life is busy. Unless you make the commitment to refuse to miss a day in praying for your children, you could easily go days without praying. Each day has 1440 minutes. If praying for your children is important, then you can find five or ten minutes in your day, can't you? So find time for them...and pray. The stakes are much too high for you to fail to pray each day for your children and their mom.

Man is never so tall as when he kneels before God—
never so great as when he humbles himself before God.
And the man who kneels to God can stand to anything.[5]

Louis H. Evans

Your children need your dual role of love and
    discipline.
Love without disciple is sentimentality.
Discipline without love is bondage.
God's dad keeps these two actions of love and
    discipline in their proper balance.

JIM GEORGE

Your rod and Your staff, they comfort me.

PSALM 23:4

A Dad Who Is a Shepherd

Shepherd the flock of God which is among you...
[not] as being lords over those entrusted to you,
but being examples to the flock.

1 PETER 5:2-3

What a year! Greg felt he had been thrust in the spiritual fast lane without a speed limit. It wasn't as if he hadn't asked for help. The birth of his little daughter had been a wake-up call for him. Looking back, he wished he'd had this wake-up call when he had married Margaret. If he'd been this serious about his marriage as he had been about his new role as a dad, the past three years would have been a lot different. Oh, it wasn't that he and Maggie (Greg's pet name for Margaret) had encountered any real problems. He had been a new believer who was willing to let his very spiritually mature wife take the lead in Christian matters. She had been a little reluctant at first, but over time, she had given in and taken the lead by default.

But now, things were definitely changing. His mentor, Bill, had been deepening Greg's understanding of Christian doctrine, and then showing Greg how these truths applied to his personal life. For the past year, Bill had been exhorting Greg to be a stronger leader in the home—in his roles as a husband and a dad. Today's mentoring lesson focused on the role of a shepherd as depicted in the Bible and its application to the role of leadership in the home.

Greg was pretty excited about this new topic because he had just witnessed firsthand a flock of sheep and a shepherd! He, Maggie, and little Mary Lou had been driving the back-country roads of Ventura County, just north of Los Angeles, and lo and behold, they had been stopped by a flock of sheep crossing the road. A shepherd and his sheep dog were guiding the flock.

Why a Shepherd?

Yes, Greg realized sheep and shepherds still exist in this modern day world. And yet the idea of shepherding is somewhat of a foreign concept for most people because they don't live in rural areas. After all, you don't come across shepherds and their sheep in Times Square in New York City, or Pershing Square in downtown Los Angeles, or the Miracle Mile of Chicago. Nor will you see them in most suburban areas either. So why use the analogy of a shepherd to help a man understand his role as a dad after God's own heart?

Shepherding Is Part of Biblical Culture

While shepherds aren't all that common in many places today, they were a big part of the agrarian world of the Bible. Even today in the Middle East herds of sheep and shepherds can be seen everywhere. They are continuing to do what they have done for thousands of years. And the job of caring for sheep is similar, in many ways, to the responsibility a dad has in caring for his children.

First let's look at some qualities about shepherds as found in the Bible. As you read along, be sure to notice how these same qualities apply to your role as a parent.

A shepherd is willing to endure hardship for his sheep—In the Old Testament, Jacob described to his uncle Laban what he had physically endured to care for Laban's sheep. "There I was! In the day the drought consumed me, and the frost by night, and my sleep departed from my eyes" (Genesis 31:40).

A shepherd is responsible for protecting his flock—David, the boy shepherd of the Old Testament, is perhaps the most well-known shepherd in Scripture. He later became the second king of Israel. Many of his psalms were written while watching his family's flocks.

Like most shepherds, David was very protective of his sheep. David even relates how he killed lions and bears while guarding over his father's sheep (see 1 Samuel 17:34-36).

A shepherd provides for his flock—The most famous psalm is Psalm 23. This well-known and often-quoted passage is often referred to as the Shepherd's Psalm. It begins with the words, "The LORD is my shepherd; I shall not want" (verse 1). In this psalm God is portrayed as a loving, caring shepherd who always provides for His flock. David, the writer of Psalm 23, viewed God's provision in a very personal way when he referred to God as "my shepherd."

The shepherd knows his flock—The use of shepherds to illustrate caring leadership continues in the New Testament and applies especially to the greatest shepherd of all, the Lord Jesus Christ. Jesus declared of Himself, "I am the good shepherd; and I know My sheep, and am known by My own" (John 10:14).

The shepherd is willing to sacrifice himself for his flock—Picture in your mind David as a young boy, with sword in hand doing battle with wild beasts as he places himself protectively in front of the sheep, willing to sacrifice himself to protect his flock. Then there is the ultimate sacrifice of the Good Shepherd, Jesus, who stated, "I am the good shepherd. The good shepherd gives His life for the sheep" (John 10:11). Jesus was the supreme shepherd—He was willing to lay down His life for His sheep. Likewise, God calls fathers to be willing to sacrifice themselves for the sake of their family.

In these biblical illustrations that mention shepherds, you can see that God has provided fathers with parallels that indicate how He desires for them to oversee their families. Much of what a shepherd did in Bible times still has application to what God calls dads to do for their families today.

The Value of a Shepherd

When it comes to dealing with his flock, a shepherd has his hands full. There's a lot to be done to protect and care for the sheep.

And children are a lot like sheep—they too need a strong guiding hand of leadership. Do you recognize the many similarities between how sheep and children need help?

> Your children may think you are overly protective... but the world is an evil place and if you aren't leading your children, then others will.

For example, sheep have no sense of their need to exercise caution—they must be led away from danger if they are to survive. Likewise, your kids are inexperienced and unaware of the evil that surrounds them. At times your children may think you are overly protective and too cautious, but the world is an evil place and if you aren't watching over your children, then others will. They will influence your children negatively or harm them. "Yea, though I walk through the valley of the shadow of death, I will fear no evil; for You are with me" (Psalm 23:4).

Sheep are totally dependent animals—to the point that they must be led to food and water. Similarly, your children need your guidance. Your leadership will be needed for as long as your children are under your roof, and possibly beyond. And hopefully they will still desire your advice when they are out on their own. "He leads me beside the still waters" (Psalm 23:2).

> God's dad is careful to keep love and discipline in their proper balance.

Sheep respond to love and sometimes need to be prodded. Your children need both your love and your discipline. Love without discipline is sentimentality. Discipline without love is bondage. God's dad is careful to keep love and discipline in their proper balance. "Your rod and Your staff, they comfort me" (Psalm 23:4).

Shepherds of the Church and You

With Jesus' ascension into heaven in Acts 1, and the birth of the church with the coming of the Holy Spirit in Acts 2, Jesus passed the shepherding of the flock on to the apostles. As the church grew and expanded to all parts of the Roman world, the apostles no longer were able to do all the shepherding of the churches by themselves. So new shepherds were appointed, and they were called elders. Several

Bible passages describe for us the responsibilities of these elders or leaders, and in these descriptions we find information that is helpful for dads who want to shepherd their own flock well.

Let's start with what the apostle Paul wrote. In Acts chapter 20, Paul was on his way to Jerusalem. Along the way he made a brief stop at Miletus and assembled the elders of the church that was nearby in Ephesus. When the elders arrived, Paul reminded them of their duties as God's shepherds.

Shepherds are to watch and warn—"after my departure savage wolves will come in among you, not sparing the flock...Therefore watch, and remember that for three years I did not cease to warn everyone night and day with tears" (verses 29,31).

Shepherds are to be servants, stewards, and examples—"Shepherd the flock of God which is among you, serving as overseers, not by compulsion but willingly, not for dishonest gain but eagerly; nor as being lords over those entrusted to you, but being examples to the flock" (1 Peter 5:2-3). Some years after Paul's speech at Miletus, Peter wrote a letter to a group of churches and referred to himself as "a fellow elder."

Are you wondering, *What do these exhortations to elders have to do with a dad being a shepherd?* If so, I'm glad you asked! In 1 Timothy 3:4, as part of the qualifications for being a shepherd of the local church, Paul told Timothy to look carefully at a man's home, to look for "one who rules his own house well, having his children in submission with all reverence." Then Paul said, "if a man does not know how to rule his own house, how will he take care of the church of God?" (1 Timothy 3:5). God's message is that leadership in the home is a requirement for being a leader in the church. Leadership in the church starts by being a leader at home.

> God values a man who is a proper shepherd of his home, his wife, and his children.

I don't know whether church leadership is of interest to you or not, but God values a man who is a proper shepherd of his home, his wife, and his children. That man is to be highly honored and is worthy of being considered for leadership. Properly shepherding your children is a biblical qualification for leadership. So let's talk more about you being a shepherd of your flock, or your family.

A Dad Feeds His Flock

Putting food on the table for your family is one of your key roles as a father. You would never think of letting your family go hungry for physical food. The church and your friends and the world would see your conduct as unthinkable. You would be considered as worse than an unbeliever, according to 1 Timothy 5:8.

So why should it be any different when it comes to spiritual food? Part of being your family's spiritual shepherd is that you are to provide spiritual food for their souls. That food can only come from one source—God's Word, the Bible.

Let's look at what Paul wrote in Acts 20. He told the elders, "I have not shunned to declare to you the whole counsel of God" (verse 27). Also, Jesus told Peter to "feed My sheep" (John 21:17). In the original Greek text of John 21:17, the word "feed" carries the idea of constantly feeding and nourishing the sheep. This was a primary duty of a shepherd in the church—to make sure his sheep (the people) had the opportunity to feed on God's Word. Likewise, as the shepherd of your children, you're to do the same. You are to make sure your children are constantly exposed to God's Word. If you take this task seriously, as you should, then you will find ways to...

- Make sure your children see you reading and studying your Bible. Make Paul's cry your own: "Imitate me, just as I also imitate Christ" (1 Corinthians 11:1).

- Make sure they take time to read their own Bibles. Remember, a good shepherd "makes" his sheep lie down and feed in green pastures (see Psalm 23:2). Again, this is where your example comes in. If your kids see how important it is for you to read and study your Bible, it will be important to them as well. A shepherd always leads the way.

- Make it a practice to have devotions with the whole family. Taking this time will reap untold spiritual blessings in the lives of your children. This practice certainly had an influence on the life of Jim Elliott, the great missionary martyr whose commitment to Christ was forged as he participated in regular devotions as a child with his family.

- Make sure your children go to church and youth group regularly. Who in your family is leading the way to faithful church attendance and involvement? Why, you are, Dad, as the leader of your flock!

- Make Christ the focal point of your conversations with your children. This will happen only if Christ is the focal point of your life.

As you purpose to make sure your children are feeding upon God's Word, don't forget to pray. Ask God daily to work through His Word and by His Spirit in your children's hearts.

A Dad Leads His Flock

Just as sheep need a leader, your family needs you to lead. Most men are involved in some form of leadership on their jobs. All day long they command, lead, and direct others toward specific goals. Even the man who works alone for the most part still has opportunities to exercise leadership or make decisions at work.

Are you practicing leadership as well in your home? What does that involve?

Leadership is a lifestyle. Something happens on the drive home from work. I can't explain it, but most of the time, when a dad opens the door to his house after commuting home, he's a different person. The person who practices leadership at work and makes decisions on a routine basis seems to have vanished. What happened?!

There is no doubt in my mind that if your house was on fire, you would lead everyone in your family to safety. You would rise to the crisis. The leadership that is so necessary in a crisis is what's needed by your family each and every day. When you come through the door of your home, the family needs to know that the leader of their family is back. Dad's home!

Every day is filled with situations which, if not dealt with properly and lovingly and decisively, could have a negative effect on your family. Granted, on a day-to-day basis, the issues you face may not seem like a big deal. But over time, if you fail to exercise ongoing leadership, the smaller problems can grow into bigger ones.

Don't let your family drift through life without a leader. Claim your God-ordained role. Wear it. Own it. Your family will be grateful for it.

Leadership follows the manual. Look to the Bible for help. To be a spiritual leader, you need spiritual maturity. In the New Testament, church leaders were chosen not because of what they knew, but because of who they were—spiritually mature men. It was their character that counted most. If you are growing spiritually and walking in obedience to God's Spirit, you will have the wisdom you need to be a godly leader for your family.

Leadership seeks advice. When you take on a new job, the boss usually pairs you with someone who has the experience to teach you how your job is to be done. It's the same way in the spiritual realm. In the same way that Bill has been mentoring Greg, you'll want a mentor who can show you how to lovingly lead your wife and children. Watch and spend time with men in your church who model strong leadership in their homes.

Leadership takes an interest. Shepherding requires your involvement in as many issues as your wife and children are facing. Some might require only a bit of your time, while others may be ongoing and take lots of time. Ask questions. Gather facts. Get advice. Formulate your thoughts for making right decisions. And pray! If in the process of dealing with an issue you develop a conviction about it, assert your role as the spiritual leader and be willing to make a decision even if it's unpopular (like saying *no* to a daughter who wants to start dating at a young age). God is not asking you to be popular. He is asking you to lead. Carry out your role both lovingly and firmly.

Leadership allows for help. Many times when a husband and father fails to assume his role as the family leader, his wife has to step in and take on the responsibility. She probably doesn't want the job, but has had to act by default. If this describes your situation, sit down with your wife and ask for her support in helping you reassume your role as leader of the family. I'm guessing you'll be greatly surprised at how happy she will be to hear your request. And it's a good practice to talk daily with your wife so that you know the issues she and the children are facing. This will help inform you on how you can best lead and care for your family.

A Dad Sacrifices for His Flock

Over the years as I have traveled and ministered extensively, I have gotten the impression that personal sacrifice is a lost art for dads. Unfortunately I meet and observe many dads who are not willing to sacrifice...

—their time for time with their children

—their interests for the interests of their children

—their fun for having fun with their children

—their comfort for the comfort of their children

—their finances for the future of their children

This is not the picture of God's plan for His shepherds of the home—His dads.

As you now know, the role of being a dad starts at the time of conception, intensifies at birth, and doesn't let up until the death of either the dad or the child. Here are a couple of my thoughts on sacrifice:

A dad is to sacrifice his time—A father should take time to teach and train and prepare his child for life. This includes time spent offering spiritual input, behavioral input, common-sense input, practical input like money management skills and wisdom for everyday life, and so on. You are called by God to guide your young prodigies as they grow into mature adults and beyond.

A dad is to sacrifice his money—A big part of raising up your children well is making sure they receive a good education and training for life. We addressed this need earlier, but we didn't talk about how much this teaching and training might cost. Your children will need to gain specific knowledge and skills that are needed for them to survive in this world, and this will likely require them to go to college or a vocational school.

When it comes to educating and training your children, you will need to plan ahead for the financial costs involved. This may mean some significant sacrifices on your part. It may mean you give up some things, or get a second job, or take on extra shifts. It may mean you don't buy a new boat, or purchase a timeshare, or take an exotic vacation.

If you start saving early, your children will have some money to at least begin college or vocational training. Doing nothing will place the financial burden squarely on your child's shoulders—and they won't be in a position to cover that cost because they'll already have a rough time as it is. So don't neglect to plan for their future. The Bible says "children should not have to save up for their parents, but parents for their children" (2 Corinthians 12:14 NIV).

You Can Do It, Dad!

Friend, I don't know your family background. I don't know if you had a dad in the home while you were growing up, if your dad was a good leader, or if maybe he was an abusive leader. But I do know that God wants *you* to lead your family. No one else on this earth can replace you as your children's dad. Your children are special, unique gifts and privileges given to you by God. And He has divinely and sovereignly placed those children in your care.

If you are feeling a little overwhelmed, or the idea of leading at home stills sounds like a foreign concept, be encouraged. God never asks you to do anything without giving you all the resources needed to accomplish it. You need His help...and He gives it. You need

His strength...and He gives it. You need His grace...and He gives it. You need His wisdom...and He gives it. God has already "given to [you] all things that pertain to life and godliness" (2 Peter 1:3). In other words, you can do it, Dad!

Small Things That Make a Big Difference

1. *Pray during your drive home from work.* This one act will help you walk in the door ready to lead—and to give of yourself to your family. You'll be focused on them instead of yourself, and you'll be ready to handle whatever is happening. And while you're praying, ask God for guidance and wisdom for shepherding your family and for any issues that are ongoing at home. The very act of praying will remind you to live out your role of shepherd.

2. *Organize daily devotions with your family.* Part of your responsibility as a shepherd is to feed your flock. If you aren't sure how to start having family devotions, read one chapter out loud from the book of Mark each day. This teaches your flock more about Jesus, their Shepherd. Family devotions are a way of ensuring that each member of the family is receiving God's Word so they can be prepared to face life's challenges and responsibilities.

3. *Talk to your children.* A good shepherd knows his sheep. What better way is there to know what's happening in your children's lives than to spend a few minutes each day with each child? A quick way to find out is to ask, "What's the hardest thing you are facing today? I want to be sure to pray about it."

4. *Talk to your wife about the children.* As part of your shepherding duties, discuss the needs of each child with your wife. Because she is probably with them more than you are, she may be able to give you valuable insights into their problems and concerns.

Be sober, be vigilant;
because your adversary the devil
walks about like a roaring lion,
seeking whom he may devour.

1 PETER 5:8

A Dad Who Is a Watchman

Therefore watch, and remember...
I did not cease to warn everyone
night and day with tears.

ACTS 20:31

Just like Proverbs 27:17 says, "Iron sharpens iron." That's how Greg viewed his weekly meetings with Bill. Yes, Bill may have been a tough Army Ranger at one time, but Greg could see why so many of the men Bill had led as a Ranger stayed in touch with him. Bill was a great leader, especially to his family. And he was a great teacher who knew how to relate spiritual truths with illustrations from his military missions.

Today was no different. As Greg and Bill continued their study of Acts 20 and the apostle Paul's speech to the leaders of the church in Ephesus, Bill recapped their previous lesson on leaders as shepherds to the church, and dads as shepherds to their families.

As their meeting progressed, the subject of being a watchman became the focus of their discussion. So it was appropriate for both Greg and Bill to share about some of the times in combat when things had gotten scary because someone had failed to properly alert the camp or fellow soldiers of impending danger. Greg commented that his base had almost been lost because the forward sentry hadn't warned everyone in time so they could properly set up a defensive position. "We were lucky to survive that attack," Greg said. "God was definitely protecting us that night!"

With that sober reflection, Bill and Greg opened their Bibles to continue their discussion of Acts 20.

The Need for a Watchman

After reading the previous chapter, I hope you are grasping your role as the shepherd of your family, which is to feed and lead your flock. In this chapter, we're going to move on and look at another function that dads must perform. You are to watch and warn. The apostle Paul described this responsibility to the Ephesian church leaders this way:

> After my departure savage wolves will come in among you, not sparing the flock. Also from among your-selves men will rise up, speaking perverse things, to draw away the disciples after themselves. Therefore watch, and remember that for three years I did not cease to warn everyone night and day with tears (Acts 20:29-31).

Paul knew the world is a desperate place, and the enemy, like sav-age wolves, is seeking to destroy the church. And, my friend, that same enemy is seeking to destroy your family. That is why you are needed to watch over your family.

The Role of a Watchman

A dad who is the spiritual leader of his family is both a shepherd and a watchman. The main function of a shepherd is to feed and lead his flock, and an additional duty he has is that of a watchman—he is to watch over his flock to protect it against predators. In Bible times, a watchmen's responsibility was to keep a vigil at the city walls and warn the inhabitants when an enemy approached or some other kind of trouble threatened.

At one point during the ministry of the Old Testament prophet Ezekiel, God appointed Ezekiel as a watchman. This meant Eze-kiel's job was to listen to any warnings God spoke to him and pass them along to the people. God told Ezekiel that when he saw the enemy, he was to blow a trumpet and warn the people (Ezekiel 33:3). If the people heard the warning but did not heed it, then the people would be responsible for the consequences of not paying attention (verse 4). However, in verse 6, God said that if a watchman failed to sound a warning to the people, then the watchman would be held accountable for any harm that came to the people.

This makes it clear that a watchman plays an important role in the safety and security of a city, or a church, or a home. With that in mind, what must he do to keep himself vigilant?

A watchman keeps himself prepared. The apostle Paul had spent three years in Ephesus shepherding a band of new believers. He had been a faithful watchman. He had paid careful attention to the enemy's tactics. He said, "I know this, that after my departure savage wolves will come in among you, not sparing the flock" (Acts 20:29).

A bit earlier, when Paul was saying farewell to the Ephesian church leaders and getting ready to move on to Jerusalem, he said, "Therefore take heed to yourselves" (Acts 20:28a). He reminded them that a good watchman needs to keep himself sharp. In this case, the Ephesian elders were to first watch over their own spiritual condition.

A watchman keeps himself informed. He knows what to look for. In World War II, spotters were placed on remote islands in the South Pacific along the flight path of Japanese planes and warships. To prepare them for their mission, the spotters were trained to identify each enemy plane and warship. This information would help them to convey appropriate warnings to others. Likewise, a father learns what to watch for so he can protect his family.

So when you consider your role as a watchman over your family, you need to watch over your own spiritual condition, and you need to develop the "spiritual eyes" that enable you to spot the potential spiritual attacks of the enemy on you and your family. If your spiritual eyes are dimmed, you won't be able to recognize the devil's schemes against you and your children. The apostle Peter describes the devil as a "roaring lion, seeking whom he may devour" (1 Peter 5:8).

Without spiritual awareness, you won't be able to watch over your family and pick out the devil's disguises and see him for who he is. If you, the watchman, are ignorant of Satan's ploys, he can wreak havoc in your life. And that, in turn, will have a negative effect on your children's lives. Both Paul and Peter's advice to you and me is that we "be sober, be vigilant" (verse 8). Be aware! A watchman knows what is required of him and what he is watching for.

Watching Takes Time

As I write about watching, I can't help but remember a particular time when Elizabeth and I had concerns about how things were going in our daughters' lives. The issues that caused our concern weren't big ones, but they were quickly recognized because we had been watching as part of our duty as parents. We worked through the minor issues, but it still took time—lots of time! Not an hour or two, but more like a month or two. Looking back, we are so glad we were on alert, noticed the problems, sounded the alarm, and took the required time to find solutions. That's what kept those small problems from escalating.

Watching takes time and attention. If you see an issue developing with any of your kids, you need to devote attention to it. Don't let your life become so busy you cannot help your children in their time of need.

What should you be looking for? Here are a few questions you should ask yourself as you watch over your children:

- What's going on in their life right now? And if something new has taken place (like a new friend, a new home in a different city), what has been its effect?

- Who are their friends, and how well do you know them?

- Have there been some negative changes in their attitudes and moods?

- Are there signs of rebellion toward you or your wife's authority?

- Are there any subtle changes in their appearance or the clothes they are now choosing to wear?

- Has their attitude about spiritual things changed?

I'm sure you can think of other questions as well. The point is, take time to observe your children. Get to know the condition of your flock. Be wise and follow this advice from Proverbs 27:23: "Be diligent to know the state of your flocks, and attend to your herds." In other words, pay attention as a good watchman.

A Watchman Warns

Noticing a negative change in behavior means you have been an alert watchman. But your job is not done yet. Once you've observed changes taking place, don't wait until it's convenient for you and your schedule to talk about the warning signs with your son or daughter. Waiting only increases the possibility that the "walls" of your child's heart have been breached by the enemy, which means you have let down your guard as a watchman.

> **Don't let your life become so busy you cannot help your children in their time of need.**

It's not enough for you to only watch for the signs that the enemy is approaching. You must also take the next steps—identify the danger, go into action, and take out the threat. Paul was very graphic in his description of what the enemy is capable of doing: "After my departure savage wolves will come in among you, not sparing the flock" (Acts 20:29).

Warning your children of impending spiritual danger is not always easily done. Your children can't see, as well as you do, the spiritual battles that are being waged around them. They don't have your vantage point as a watchman on top of the wall—they don't have your knowledge and experience about the dangers that can come their way. Therefore they may respond to you by saying, "Why are you so uptight? Why can't you let me have some fun? What's wrong with my friends? Why do I have to go to church?"

These are the times when you absolutely must lead. You must "take up the full armor of God, that you [and your child] will be able to resist in the evil day, and having done everything, stand firm" (Ephesians 6:13 NASB). When your child is in spiritual danger, your love and role as a watchman requires that you act. What are some steps you can take to warn your children?

— Start by telling them that your love for them is what compels you to warn them of these spiritual dangers.

—Review the plan of salvation. If they are true believers in Christ and born again in Him, then they need to want and seek to act like God's children.

—Show them in the Bible what's wrong with what they are doing or wanting to do.

—Don't let them shut you out. Graciously persist in talking through the changes you are seeing.

—Don't give in to their desire to rebel. Pray with them about their life and God's will.

—Assign Bible passages for them to read—passages that deal with rebellion and disobedience (1 Samuel 15:22-23).

—Discuss their choice of friends and any negative influences that others are having on their life.

—Demonstrate your resolve to do daily battle for their soul and for as long as it takes for them to come around.

It's not at all easy being "the wet blanket" or "the bad guy" in the eyes of your children. But because you love them, you will be willing to take a firm stand when it comes to their spiritual protection.

Here's what one Bible commentator wrote about the apostle Paul in connection with the words of warning he spoke to the Ephesian elders in Acts 20 (by the way, this was written under the subtitle "No Shrinking Violets"):

> [Paul] understood that there can be no growth in Christ without the transmission of truth. Are you fulfilling your God-given responsibility to declare God's truth to those he has sovereignly placed in your life— a spouse, a neighbor, a child? Or are you hesitating and shrinking back from such a task? The only way to have a clear conscience is to trust God and boldly speak out...[1]

Living Out Your Watchman's Role

I don't know what stage of parenting you are in now, but don't ever lose heart. Hang in there. The rewards for living out your watchman's role with tenacity will be great not only now, but for a lifetime to come, and beyond. Also, be encouraged. Others have gone before you and have also faced some of the same concerns you have. Do like Elizabeth and I did when we had concerns, and seek advice from others. Don't be too proud to ask for help. The problem might not be as serious as you think, and the reassurance of others will strengthen you for even bigger battles as your children continue to mature.

And speaking of advice: One dad gave Elizabeth and me the analogy of parenting as a game of football being played on the field. He said there are three basic kinds of parents:

The 50-yard-line parents—Some parents take their children to the 50-yard line and walk away. This would be sometime during the high school years. They would say to their kids, "You are old enough to know what is right and what is wrong. Don't get into any trouble. Good luck!"

The 10-yard-line parents—Other parents take their children all the way through high school graduation to the 10-yard line. In the parents' mind, their responsibility is finished. They tell their children, "You're 18 years old now—you're old enough to make your own decisions. You are now on your own. Make us proud!"

The across-the-goal-line parents—Then there are the wise parents who take their children all the way across the goal line. They stay alongside their kids for however long it takes to properly prepare them to flourish both physically and spiritually. This may continue all through college, up to marriage, or up to some other point, but in every case, they make an all-the-way commitment. And in most cases, the children are glad for their parents' continued interest and encouragement in their lives.

Entrust Your Children to God

Can I give you an understatement? *Parenting is one of the hardest things you will ever do.* It's not easy. In fact, it is downright hard! But...

if you will hang in there with God,
if you will do your part in raising your children for God,
if you will hang in there with your kids,
if you will resist the pressures of society,

...then you will experience incredible blessing from your children. But you must do your part just as the apostle Paul did with the Ephesian church leaders. In the same way that the apostle Paul alerted the elders about protecting the flock, you are to stand alert in your care of your children. How can you do this?

Trust in prayer—Paul told the Ephesian elders, "I commend you to God" (Acts 20:32). Paul was devoted to praying for them. In fact, he spent his life praying not only for these people, but for all the churches.[2]

As a parent, you have likely spent a lot of time focused on your children. From the moment of conception, you began devoting attention to them. You started by decorating their rooms. You initiated your watchman's role by making sure you lived in a safe neighborhood. You did your research and found which neighborhoods have the best schools. You've made sure your children are well-rounded by giving them piano, gymnastic, and swimming lessons and letting them participate in little league and soccer. And of course, you've given them a good home life. You've raised them, fed them, protected them, trained them. But in the final analysis, even your best human attempts at being a watchman cannot overcome the effects of any lack of praying you do on their behalf. Why?

> There is no substitute for your impassioned prayers on behalf of your children.

Because prayer speaks of dependence on God. Hopefully your human efforts at watching and warning will help produce children who will turn out well. But only prayer can help you raise a child after God's own heart. There is no substitute for your impassioned prayers on behalf of your children. That's because prayer expresses reliance upon God and acknowledges your trust in Him to work in the hearts of your children.

If you want to trust God with your children's future, then you must place them in God's merciful hands through daily prayer.

Trust in God's Word—Paul first entrusted the church leaders in Ephesus "to God" in his prayers, but then added "and to the word of His grace" (verse 32). Though prayer is essential, it must be paired with obedience to God's Word. Paul set the Ephesian church leaders before God in prayer, and here in verse 32 he sets the Bible before them. Like a waiter who brings food to people waiting at a restaurant table, Paul placed God's Word before the Ephesian elders during his time with them.

He now trusts God that as the leaders in Ephesus continue to study the Word, their spiritual watchfulness will stay vigilant. Yes, savage wolves hover about, but Paul trusts that God's Word will keep his beloved friends safe and "build [them] up" spiritually.[3]

Paul's trust in the power of God's Word should give you—as a physical and spiritual father—a model to follow. Pray for your children—for their salvation and spiritual growth and maturity. And remember that God's Word is your guidebook for parenting. You are not just raising children for the sake of getting them to adulthood. Rather, you are raising children who hopefully and prayerfully will grow up to become mature believers who reflect Jesus in their actions and attitudes. Then, whether your grown children are working at a job, or at home with their own children, or engaging with others in their community, they will radiate the love of Jesus to a needy world.

You Can Do it, Dad!

Watching is one thing. Even a teacher or stranger can notice if or when your kids are in trouble. But only you can move beyond what you observe in your children to correcting what you are seeing. Be strong, Dad. Own your role as a watchman. Realize how important both prayer and the Word of God are in the parenting process. As Paul told Timothy, his son in the faith, "all Scripture…is profitable… for reproof, for correction, for instruction in righteousness." The purpose of encouraging your children to get into God's Word is so "that the man of God may be complete, thoroughly equipped for every good work" (2 Timothy 3:16-17).

Isn't it reassuring that through all the days and nights of watching over your children and actively pointing them toward God you are preparing to launch men or women after God's own heart into the world? As you are faithful to instill God's Word into their lives and hearts, they will possess the resources they need to guard themselves and ultimately watch and warn over their own future families.

Small Steps That Make a Big Difference

1. *Build a wall around your family.* Throughout the centuries, people built walls around their cities and homes to protect themselves. Without those walls, the people and their homes were vulnerable. The walls kept danger out—and because they were high, they also provided a great vantage point for detecting an enemy from a distance.

As a dad, your duty is to be an alert watchman. Build the wall as high as you can around the family you love. Build it on the bedrock of loyalty to the Lord and His standards. Then, as your title of *watchman* signifies, watch for any approaching enemies that might endanger your flock.

2. *Build a solid prayer life.* Perhaps you're not a prayer warrior who cloisters himself away for multiple hours a day in prayer. But you can be a dad who routinely takes five or ten minutes each day to fervently pray for your children, their mother, and their home. And as you go through your day, take frequent looks at a picture of your family on your phone or on your desk at work or in your carry-on as you travel. Praying for your children doesn't take up a lot of time, but your petitions can stretch through a 24-hour day as you shoot "arrow prayers" up to God for each of your loved ones.

3. *Watch over your children's friendships.* Next to you as a parent, friends have the greatest influence in your kids' lives. Be sure to invite their friends over and take an up-close and personal look at who your children are spending time with. While you are watching over their

friendships, teach your children how to choose the right kind of friends. Help each child make a list of qualities that are biblical and desirable in a friend. (Hint: The book of Proverbs is explicit in telling young people exactly what kind of friends to have—and not have.)

A watchman's job is routine
until the enemy is spotted.

I will instruct you and teach you
in the way you should go;
I will guide you with my eye.

PSALM 32:8

(10)

A Dad Who Is a Guide

When David had served God's purpose
in his own generation, he fell asleep.

ACTS 13:36 (NIV)

Besides being a spiritually mature Christian, a loving husband, and an incredible father, Greg's mentor, Bill, was also ex-Army like Greg. During one of their recent meetings, Bill had given Greg another one of the brief glimpses he often shared about his years as an Army Ranger. Ever the teacher, Bill sometimes used war stories to illustrate spiritual truths to Greg. Today, as Bill looked off into the distance, he told Greg about a time when his Ranger platoon had been inserted at night into a hostile tribal area in Afghanistan. Their objective was to seize a village controlled and captured by several high-ranking Taliban leaders. The operation was a success because there had been a lot of pre-mission planning. But also key to their success was the fact his squad had the help of a guide who knew the area well and led them to their objective.

Bill then turned to Greg and said, "You are like that guide on our mission. Your little daughter needs you to direct her to her objective, to show her the way to fulfill God's purpose for her life."

Fulfilling God's Purpose

While it's not possible to know the future that awaits your children, you *can* guide them toward the future God intends for them—His purpose for their lives. Just as Bill's guide in Afghanistan helped to make his squad's mission successful, so can you help your children to walk in the right direction so they are able to fulfill their purpose.

What got me thinking about God's purpose came to mind as I was reading Acts 13:22 in the NIV translation: "David son of Jesse [is] a man after my own heart; he will do everything I want him to do." I read on to finish chapter 13 and reached verse 36, which speaks of God's purpose: "When David had served God's purpose in his own generation, he fell asleep."

There it was, staring me in the face. A man or a dad after God's own heart fulfills God's purpose! Did you know you have a purpose? As a child of God, you have a destiny. God has a plan for you. Hopefully you desire to find out what that purpose is. And what is that purpose? Well, for example, if you have children, then you know that part of God's plan includes you as a father facilitating the training of your children (Deuteronomy 6:6-7; Proverbs 22:6.)

Just as your personal goal is to "serve the purpose of God" as a father, you are also to help your children along the way to finding God's purpose for their lives. What an amazing privilege you have, pointing your children to God so they might allow Him to unfold His purpose for each of them.

How can you guide your children toward knowing God's purpose for them? There are several "lifestyle practices" they can put to work in their own lives that, over time, will allow God to direct their path. Let's find out what these lifetime practices are:

Practice #1: Be a Reader

Reading is the window to all learning. Encourage your children to be readers. That will expose them to the world and the knowledge and experiences of others. God told Joshua exactly how to carry out God's mission for him:

> This Book of the Law shall not depart from your mouth, but you shall meditate in it day and night, that you may observe to do according to all that is written in it. For then you will make your way prosperous, and then you will have good success (Joshua 1:8).

Joshua was told to read God's laws, meditate on them, and obey them. Then he would be successful in God's eyes. This is good advice for both parents and children. If you want to be wise and want your children to be wise, be sure to read the wisdom of others, especially the wisdom found in the Bible.

Wisdom and knowledge don't come without effort. A big part of that effort involves reading. Unfortunately, varied statistics show that men buy far fewer books than women. It's common to hear Christian publishing professionals say that women buy about 80 percent of all Christian books sold, while men buy only about 20 percent.

It's as simple as this: If you don't see reading as important, then your children probably won't either. You yourself need to be convinced that being a reader is an important part of growing both spiritually and mentally. Only as you model this to your children will they become readers.

Perhaps you don't like to read. You never have. And maybe you don't read because you have trouble trying to do so. But it doesn't have to be that way. Reading is just like any other skill. How do you learn a skill? You start from the beginning and develop the skill as you go. Start by picking books about subjects that you are highly interested in—history, health, a hobby. Or start reading books that help you solve a problem you're struggling with—like how to better manage your time, how to be a better salesman, how to be a better husband and dad.

If finances are tight and you don't have the money to buy books, then go to your local public library—it is a goldmine of wisdom! And if the library doesn't have the book you're looking for, you can ask them to obtain it from another library.

Once you begin to make reading a habit, you'll discover the truth of the statement, "Reading is to the mind what exercise is to the body."[1] A good way to start up is to set a goal of reading one chapter a day. Set aside time to make that happen—like during your lunch hour, or during your visit to a coffee shop.

To help you remember what you learn, go ahead and mark up the book. Underline the portions that stood out to you, or make notes in the margin or inside the back cover of the book. In these ways, you'll train yourself to better retain important information.

And don't forget—the *first* book you want to read and have your children read is the Bible. Find a translation that you like, that's easy for you to read and understand. It's okay if you decide to use the same translation your children are reading.

Practice #2: Be a Learner

As your children become more active as readers, they will find themselves constantly learning new things. What better way to spend part of your dinner time as a family than to let your children share what they are discovering in their books? You'll be thrilled when one of your children says, "Here's something really cool I read today."

As a dad, you want to help your children realize that school isn't the only place for learning. Rather, learning is a state of mind, an attitude. It can take place anytime. Help your children to realize...

> learning is progressive—it builds upon itself.
> learning is not dependent on your IQ.
> learning does not distinguish between races.
> learning does not require a formal classroom.
> learning does not require a degree.[2]

Again, learning is an attitude. And you can instill this attitude in your children as you guide them into all sorts of learning experiences, like visiting museums and aquariums, watching educational DVDs and the History Channel, exploring new places during your vacations. As your children learn, don't forget to relate their new learning to God Himself. Include God in the picture. Deuteronomy 6:7 exhorts parents to "talk of them [God's wonders and creation]... when you walk [with your children] by the way."

Practice #3: Be Diligent

Teaching your children to be diligent will propel them down the path of fulfilling God's purpose. In fact, this is what God desires for us to do. Colossians 3:17 says, "Whatever you do in word or deed, do all in the name of the Lord Jesus." This exhortation is repeated in 1 Corinthians 10:31: "Whether you eat or drink, or whatever you do, do all to the glory of God."

In a personal letter about Timothy's pastoral duties, the apostle Paul admonished his young disciple to "be diligent to present yourself approved to God, a worker who does not need to be ashamed, rightly dividing the word of truth" (2 Timothy 2:15). Here, Paul acted as a father to his son in the faith and encouraged him to be diligent. One Bible commentator explained: "Consistent and diligent study of God's Word is vital; otherwise we will be lulled into neglecting God and our true purpose for living."[3]

God is asking you to develop this same kind of diligence in whatever you do. To be the best, and do the best. For fame or fortune? No, for the glory of God. You represent Christ. If you do this at home as a parent, or at church, or in your job, guess what? You will be a major positive influence in all these spheres. Best of all, your children will admire and emulate you.

You can't force your children to be diligent, but you can model diligence for them. At every opportunity instill this biblical practice into their hearts and minds. Start now, no matter what their age. It's never too early or too late to model and teach diligence in all areas of life.

Practice #4: Be a Servant

As a Christian, you are to approach everything in life as a servant. This applies to your involvement at church, your attitude in the workplace, and especially to your roles at home as a husband and dad. Jesus used Himself as an example to help us understand what it means to be a servant. Read on.

> As a Christian, you are to approach everything in life as a servant.

A week or so before His death, Jesus and His disciples were on their way to Jerusalem. Along the way, two of His disciples, James and his brother John, asked Jesus to give them special places of honor in Christ's future kingdom. How did Jesus reply?

> You know that the rulers of the Gentiles lord it over them, and those who are great exercise authority over them. Yet it shall not be so among you; but whoever desires to become great among you, let him be your

servant. And whoever desires to be first among you, let him be your slave—just as the Son of Man did not come to be served, but to serve, and to give His life a ransom for many (Matthew 20:25-28).

Do you want your children to be "great"—that is, prominent or powerful—or do you want them to be a positive influence? Then guide them toward being humble, helpful servants. How is this to be done? By modeling servanthood yourself. Set an example your children can't shake. This requires that you understand what a servant looks like.

A servant has a humble posture. Pride, arrogance, and a "better than thou" attitude are foreign concepts to a servant. Point your children to Jesus. Show them scriptures that teach them not to think or act like they are better than others. Show them Jesus as seen in this powerful Bible passage: "Let nothing be done through selfish ambition or conceit, but in lowliness of mind let each esteem others better than himself. Let each of you look out not only for his own interests, but also for the interests of others" (Philippians 2:3-5).

Then Paul continued, "Let this mind be in you which was also in Christ Jesus," who, even though He was God in human flesh, He "humbled Himself and became obedient to the point of death" (Philippians 2:5,8).

A servant asks—not tells. How a person speaks betrays the heart. A person—and a dad—who doesn't *demand* but *asks* models a respectful attitude toward the people he addresses. As a boss, husband, or father, you may think your credibility as a leader demands rough, authoritative "barks" and directives. However, Jesus, as a Jew, did not demand a drink of water from someone the Jews considered an inferior person—a Samaritan and a woman. He didn't command, "Get Me a drink." Rather, He asked, "Give Me a drink." Astonished, the Samaritan woman said, "How is it that You, being a Jew, ask a drink from me, a Samaritan woman?" (John 4:7,9).

Respect must be earned. Try toning down your orders to your brood at home and see what happens. This is a lesson you most definitely want your children to learn.

A servant gives, and doesn't take. Taking is natural. It's selfish, and it's the attitude of self-perseveration. Many of the people you meet at work or other places have a common characteristic—they are takers. They believe you and others around them are there to serve them, promote them, cover for them, and help them out. They take your time, your energy, your ideas, and anything else they can get out of you.

There's another word for this—*selfishness*. It's a part of the sinful human nature. And guess what? I'm sure you've realized that your children started out as takers from Day One. This is where you, Dad, and your wife come in. Your job as Christian parents is to guide your children away from selfish behavior. You are to train them to be givers and not takers, and the best way to do this is to model it in your own lives.

You may have heard this challenge before: Always leave a place or people better than when you found them. I've tried to follow this axiom ever since I first heard it. This life-principle is the definition of giving! What a terrific attitude to possess. This can be as simple as turning out the light as you leave a room, or putting your empty shopping cart in its designated place, or never leaving a person without a word of encouragement or a helping hand. In all that you do, give freely, generously, expecting nothing in return.

Imagine how modeling this attitude will benefit your children. Think about how you can give to them as you are driving home each day from work. Time? Love? Attention? Advice? A shoulder to cry on? A person or a family in need? The list for giving opportunities is limitless. Your focus on giving will encourage your children to become givers.

Practice #5: Seek the Higher Road

Are you still wondering what God's purpose is for you and your children? Well, it's certainly not "just getting by," or taking the easy way out or making excuses. These actions are what people often call "taking the lower road."

The lower road is well traveled because it's easy.
The lower road offers few challenges and therefore produces little or no growth.

The lower road provides a comfort zone that frees its travelers from the tensions that can produce growth.

The lower road offers many opportunities for self-gratification and scoffs at self-control.

The lower road gives the appearance of offering the greatest rewards for the least effort.

The lower road is all downhill.

This lower road sounds pretty good, doesn't it? So why should you take the higher road and guide your children on it as well?

The higher road is always the more difficult path. It's less traveled. Fewer people attempt it. But it always leads to God's best.

The higher road offers the greatest opportunities for growth and development.

The higher road is difficult in the beginning, but with travel and experience becomes easier.

The higher road, though difficult, produces excellence, while the lower road produces indolence.

The higher road has many biblical examples, such as...

Abraham—He left his home country not knowing where he was going.

Moses—He chose to leave the king's court.

Ruth—She chose to leave her family and country to serve Israel's God.

Jesus—He left the perfection of heaven to suffer and die for the sins of mankind.

The Twelve Disciples—They chose to leave their families and businesses to follow Jesus.

Paul—He chose to follow Christ and suffer a lifetime of persecution, difficult travels, and martyrdom.

Finally, the higher road, the road of excellence, leaves no regrets. One of the most compelling reasons to seek the higher road is that the lower road is Satan's favorite road. It's the road he offered to:

Eve—Rather than take the high road of obedience and do what God said—do not eat "of the tree of the knowledge of good and evil"—she listened to Satan, who said, "God knows that in the day you eat of it your eyes will be opened, and you will be like God, knowing good and evil" (Genesis 2:17; 3:5).

Achan—When the Israelites prepared to do battle against Ai, they were told not to take any of the spoils of battle because the spoils belonged to God (always the high road). But Achan saw some silver and gold and took it for himself (the low road—see Joshua chapter 7).

Jesus—Three times the devil offered the low road to Jesus after He had completed 40 days of fasting in the wilderness:

> "If You are the Son of God, command that these stones become bread" (Matthew 4:3).

> "If You are the Son of God, throw Yourself down. For it is written: 'He shall give His angels charge over you'" (verse 6).

> "Again, the devil took Him up on an exceedingly high mountain, and showed Him all the kingdoms of the world and their glory. And he said to Him, 'All these things I will give You if You will fall down and worship me'" (verses 8-9).

Ananias and Sapphira—sold some land and, for whatever reason, chose to take the low road and to lie about the transaction as they gave a partial gift to the church. Peter asked, "Why has Satan filled your heart to lie...?" (Acts 5:3).

All of what we've talked about in this chapter leads us back to you, dad, and your role as a guide. A guide is committed to helping the people he leads to reach their targeted objective. Along the way, he is ever aware of the environment and any potential dangers. To accomplish his task, a guide must be physically and mentally fit for the job. That's what God is asking of you as a father—that you be dedicated to living as this kind of guide for your children.

You Can Do It, Dad!

What are you thinking as you consider God's call for you to be a guide for your children?

That it's a lot of work? Yes, it is.

That it's a huge responsibility? Yes, it is.

That it's going to take some time? Yes again.

But even with this reality check, surely you can also say, "Wow, what a great privilege!"

Let's return to Bill's recollections of what happened during that mission in Afghanistan. Bill credited a great deal of the success of that mission to an expert guide. What if Bill's guide hadn't really known what he was doing or where he was going? The mission would probably have turned out a lot differently!

In your role as a dad, God is asking you to be a faithful, knowledgeable guide to guide your children. And the objective is to help your children find God's purposes for their lives. That's your goal.

Because every child is unique, you'll probably have to take each child on a slightly different path. But you must always keep God's ultimate purpose as your goal and focus. Above all else, don't take the easy way out and lead your children down the low road. And worse, don't let indifference, laziness, or a lack of effort on your part put them on the low road by default. You are your children's God-appointed guide.

What greater gift can you give your children than a dad who knows the mission objective, who doesn't compromise, who doesn't take shortcuts, who shuns the low road, and who always accepts the challenge to do better and be better? Stay close to your guide—to God Himself. Ask Him to train you to be the best guide you can possibly be. Be a guide who leads his family on the higher road that leads to Christlike character here and now while heading toward an eternal life lived in the presence of God forever and ever.

Small Steps That Make a Big Difference

1. *Know your purpose.* What is God's will for your life? Greg had a mentor who could help him on his journey. If you don't know where you are going, then you can't guide your family. Your first purpose is to know God yourself. Then you can help your children find the path that moves them toward Jesus. In the same way you are following God's path and plan, "train up [your] child in the way he should go" (Proverbs 22:6).

2. *Start with the basics.* Every child needs to be taught and trained in the basics such as discipline, obedience, love for God and family. If rebellion and self-indulgence take root in a child, then he will probably not be interested in God's purpose for his life.

3. *Treat each child individually.* A wise, effective trail guide knows the physical condition of each person he's guiding. In the same way, you must know the various strengths, weaknesses, personalities, and abilities of each of your children. Guide each child on the path toward his or her own future, not the path that a sibling is on. As Psalm 139:14 says, each one is "fearfully and wonderfully made," and his or her path will be different and unique. It's your job, Dad, to help each of your children find their special path—God's path for them, God's purpose.

*Your word is a lamp to my feet
and a light to my path.*

PSALM 119:105

You will find, if you think for a moment,
that the people who influence you
are the people who believe in you.[2]

HENRY DRUMMOND

A Dad Who Is an Encourager

When we could no longer endure it,
we thought it good to be left in Athens alone, and
sent Timothy... to establish you and
encourage you concerning your faith.

1 Thessalonians 2:1-2

Greg's cell phone buzzed. The readout displayed Bill's number, which surprised Greg. Usually it was Greg who was calling Bill, his mentor.

"This is Greg."

"Good afternoon," said Bill. He had called Greg at his workplace, which was even more unusual. Greg's curiosity was piqued.

"What's up, Bill?" Greg asked.

"Greg, as you know, I'm coaching a boys' and girls' soccer team, and I wanted to ask if you could join me for the team's practice session on Thursday. Can you make it?"

"Sure!" Greg didn't even hesitate. He valued every minute he could spend with Bill. If that meant watching children run around and play soccer, then there must be something Bill wanted him to learn.

On Thursday, after an hour of watching the little guys and gals kick the ball up and down the field with occasional slips, falls, and looks of bewilderment, Bill came over to Greg. "Greg, do you see that young boy over there?" Bill asked as he pointed to an under-sized child. Bill continued, "All these boys and girls are my projects, but young Timmy is my special assignment. He has a rough home life and gets very little support or encouragement. Many of the parents of these kids express disappointment when their children don't exhibit strong athletic potential. Unfortunately, these parents don't realize the value of encouragement.

"Most people assume my job as coach is to get these kids to win games. But I believe my most important task is to be an encourager to each and every one of these kids. I want to send them home after practice or a game feeling like at least one person in the world thinks they are special and believes in them.

"Greg, I know you're still new in your role as a parent, but I hope you'll remember what I'm trying to do for these kids. That's the kind of father you need to be for your daughter. Don't be a dad who sees only what your daughter *can't* do. Instead, see what she *can* do. Be your daughter's biggest fan!"

Everyone Needs Encouragement

When it comes to cheering people on, we tend to think in terms of coaches, cheerleaders, pep squads, and fans rooting for a favorite athletic team. But *everyone* needs encouragement. You and I need encouragement from others, and others need it from us. Consider, for example, the following scenario:

You wake up to a new day, filled with all the hope and promise of joy, accomplishment, and fulfillment. Why? Because you've been working long and hard on a really big project, and you're almost done. You worked late the night before, came home late to catch a few hours of sleep, and then quickly showered this morning before going to work to present the results of your labors to your boss. You had poured your heart into this project, and you were satisfied that you had done your best.

But when you presented your work to your boss, rather than thank you or give you any words of encouragement, your boss quickly glanced at what you had done and dismissed you without even a comment. You know you're expected to perform well for your job, but your boss's lack of even a bit of appreciation for your hard work is devastating. Talk about sticking a pin in your balloon!

There are other scenarios that can bring discouragement your way as well. For example, keeping up with the care of a child who has a disability. Dealing with a parent whose health is rapidly declining. The threat of being laid off because of downsizing within your company. Don't tell me at times you couldn't use a little encouragement!

Well, the same is true of your children! Even though the difficulties they face may be of a smaller scale, still, to them, their problems may seem overwhelming. When they are struggling, a hug or word of encouragement can go a long way toward giving them much-needed confidence and hope.

Jesus Offers Us Encouragement

Times of disappointment, discouragement, and despair are part of life. In my years of ministry, I've talked with many men who have revealed the wear and tear they've endured as they've faced various serious difficulties. Whenever I encounter one of these beat-down and brokenhearted guys, I usually share what Jesus told His disciples on the night before His crucifixion as they began to realize He was leaving them:

> These things I have spoken to you, that in Me you may
> have peace. In the world you will have tribulation; but
> be of good cheer, I have overcome the world (John
> 16:33).

Here's an encouraging truth: Jesus knew His disciples, and He knows you today. What does He know? That often you are tempted to throw your hands up in despair and feel like quitting when life gets unbearably demanding and difficult. Jesus said we would experience troubles. But He also did three things for His disciples to encourage them, and He offers this same encouragement to you today.

Let's look more closely at John 16:33. Notice that Jesus' encouragement wasn't couched in any form of symbolism or half-truths. No, He reached out to His disciples and addressed the reality they will face hardship. Then He reminded them of how they are to respond. His wonderful words of encouragement still apply today, to you and any "tribulation" you encounter.

First, Jesus declared the bad news. He said, "You will have tribulation." Yes, you will experience difficulties in this life. Things won't always go your way. Aren't you glad Jesus was honest? You can pray, "Thank You, Lord Jesus, that having already experienced grief to its max, You understand my situation."

The knowledge that life is not always fair or easy—and the fact Jesus stands ready to help—should prepare you to gently encourage your children as they face their struggles.

Second, Jesus proclaimed the good news. He is the answer to life's tribulations. It doesn't matter what you are facing, Jesus is your sure source of encouragement: "Be of good cheer, I have overcome the world."

As you know full well, we live in dangerous times. Hatred, violence, crime, and betrayal surround us. Your children are not immune to their surroundings, no matter how you try to shelter them. Have you faithfully communicated to them that Jesus is the answer to the problems they encounter? Encourage them by sharing John 16:33—by telling them the good news that Jesus is in charge and has overcome the world.

Third, Jesus provided the outcome of encouragement—peace. He began verse 33 by stating the result of His encouragement: "These things I have spoken to you, that in Me you may have peace." The Prince of Peace knew that difficult times were coming, and He offered His followers encouragement that would help calm them and give them peace of mind. He assured them that He had all things under His control.

Jesus knew what His disciples would face and encouraged them. Likewise, you know what kinds of difficulties your children will face. Don't fail to encourage them at every opportunity. Point them to Jesus—to His sovereign control over all things, and to the peace He gives.

Finally, Jesus showed us how to encourage others. There are many ways to offer encouragement, but the chief method is modeled for us when Jesus says, "These things I have *spoken* to you." Jesus encouraged through His words. He spoke words of encouragement.

I'm sure you can recall a time when you were suffering or anxious or in pain. And then someone came alongside you and gave you a smile, a listening ear, and perhaps a hug or a slap on the back, then spoke words that helped to lift your spirits. Those words meant a lot to you and enabled you to keep moving forward in spite of your circumstances.

Throughout the Gospels, Jesus spoke words of encouragement. "These things I have spoken to you." Jesus is our rock-solid example. With His help, we are to speak words that point to truths from the Bible—words that comfort, that motivate, that compel others to keep on keeping on in their desire to live for Christ. We're to speak words that encourage others to live in a way that honors Jesus.

Dad, who better can you speak encouraging words to than your children? Your words can give hope, impart faith, and empower your children to keep trying. To never give up. To trust the Lord. You've experienced Jesus' words of encouragement yourself. Now make sure to pass them on. Help your children know the relief, courage, and energy that come only in trusting what Jesus can offer. Your words of encouragement to your children can fan the flame of faith, a flame that nothing can extinguish.

Keep all that in mind as you encourage your family: A dad after God's own heart models Christ's peace. What is your normal response when your boss doesn't show his appreciation for a job well done? Do you take out your frustration on others, such as your coworkers, and ultimately your family? Do you go home, slam the door, kick the dog, yell at your sweet wife, and ignore your kids?

When you act like this, what is the result? You have allowed the world to adversely affect one of the most precious things you possess—your family. Jesus' encouragement in John 16:33 could be stated this way: "Don't let life's tribulations affect your walk with Me. Don't let the world take away your peace."

> Your words can give hope, impart faith, and empower your children to keep trying.

Take Jesus' assurance of His peace to heart. And in spite of what's going on around you, walk into your home with Christ's peace. Kiss your wife, ask your children how their day went, and be nice to the family pets.

Do you want to be an encouragement to your family? Then start by modeling Christ's peace. Don't let the world rob you of that peace. Radiate the "peace of God, which surpasses all understanding" (Philippians 4:7). Your serenity will be an encouragement to your family before you say a word. Your calm spirit will calm their spirits, and together with Jesus and as a family, you can work through any problems that have come up.

How to Be Your Children's #1 Encourager

God never gives you an assignment without also giving you the grace and the means to carry it out! As I considered about the how-tos of being your children's #1 supporter, it occurred to me that the most important rule for being an encourager is to make sure all your encouragement is authentic and from your heart. To do this, you need to prepare yourself by making a few key decisions:

Decision #1

Set a daily goal of seeking encouragement first thing from God's Word. You want and need to be a positive husband and father, and there's no better place to start that journey than in God's Word. You cannot impart what you do not possess. Look what happened when the prophet Jeremiah experienced the power of God's Word: "Your words were found, and I ate them, and Your word was to me the joy and rejoicing of my heart" (Jeremiah 15:16).

What child wouldn't love to have this kind of dad—a dad who's filled with the positive and powerful energy and joy only God can supply? So dig into God's Word on a daily basis. Go a step farther and mark every verse you find that brings you fresh confidence in God's plan or wisdom or sovereignty regarding life's challenges. You can even code them in the margins of your Bible so you can quickly find encouragement from God when you need it. And don't forget to share these verses with your wife and children so they too can know the same confidence, wisdom, and strength for their days.

Once you have strengthened yourself, you can turn your mind

away from self and focus on others, especially your family. They need you to be available as a source of strength and support. In the Old Testament, King David asked, "Where does my help come from?" The answer? "My help comes from the LORD, the Maker of heaven and earth" (Psalm 121:1-2 NIV).

The Lord's help is there for you too. God speaks directly to you right in your Bible. So bless yourself by soaking up God's help and hope...and then bless your wife and children by being a source of strength for them as they trek through life.

Decision #2

Make the effort to memorize specific Bible verses that will encourage you and others. This is the next step beyond just reading God's Word. Once you find verses that are particularly encouraging to you, commit them to memory. We've already talked about reading your Bible and memorizing Scripture passages, and this is an especially good reason to do so. You'll always be thankful for every verse you memorize because once you have deposited God's truths and promises into your mind, you can turn to them anytime and anywhere. They become your personal on-the-spot encouragers that lift you up.

When you have God's gems of strength stored away in your mind, you are able to pass them on to your children. You can give them the wisdom of the ages. You can share God's personal take on each situation they face. At the first sign of discouragement or downheartedness in one of them, you can go to that child and give real help.

> When you have God's gems of strength stored away in your mind, you are able to pass them on to your children.

This is such an easy, natural way to teach God's truth to your children. You can help them through hard times and show them how to turn to God and draw on His strength. And the big plus is that it's *God's* Word you are sharing, not man's. You are depositing God's living Word into your children's hearts. Then it's always there for them to draw upon when you're not available.

Decision #3

Take every opportunity to encourage your children. God's instruction to His people is that they be sure to "encourage one another and build each other up" (1 Thessalonians 5:11 NIV). These words are also translated "comfort each other and edify one another" (NKJV).

The primary way you can encourage your children is through your spoken words. You can share Bible verses with them, or offer helpful thoughts or wise advice. In these ways, you can provide encouragement to your children.

Encouragement can also be communicated through writing— you can write a note, a letter, an email, or even a brief text message or Tweet with the goal of offering hope to a child who is suffering or struggling. The Bible says you are to "comfort the fainthearted" (1 Thessalonians 5:14 NKJV), or "encourage the disheartened" (NIV).

Encouragement Is a Ministry

Here's another challenge: Purpose to encourage everyone you talk to. Put this goal on your prayer list and pray each day that you would remember to think of some truth from the Bible that you can pass on to those who are hurting.

And guess who should be at the top of your prayer list? Guess who should get the first overflow of your ministry of encouragement? Your family! I realize this doesn't come naturally for most guys. You may find that takes effort and practice and an act of your will to open your mouth and let God's Word minister to others. But the results are well worthwhile.

As a dad of a bustling household with two daughters, here's one thing I began to do each morning: I purposefully began to think about the first words I would speak to my family members as they prepared for school, work, or whatever they were facing that day. After all, they would be facing difficulties every day while they were "out there" away from home. I wanted to help start their day on a positive note with encouragement.

Your thoughtful, prepared words will be powerful enough to set the sail for their day. Your parting words filled with affirming, uplifting, and memorable encouragement will carry them through the more trying moments of the day. So much so that your family can fall back on your words even in the days, months, and years to come when things get tough!

Think about it: In one day at home or at school, there's a long list of possible difficulties or failures your family might face. For example, your wife might have a boss who's hard to please. Your children may be challenged by their peers because of their Christian beliefs. And everyone in your family is vulnerable to people who make comments that hurt.

Perhaps you have a preschooler who isn't as fast at learning the alphabet or in running a race as someone else. It would be easy for your child to just stop trying and withdraw. Or maybe your grade-schooler is laughed at because his or her lunch isn't as special as what the other kids have. Or maybe your tenth-grader was called on to respond to a question and didn't know what to say, or worse, gave the wrong answer! Whatever the situation, it's tough for kids when they are embarrassed or ridiculed in front of others.

That's when it's important for you to come along and, with a few positive words from the Bible, explain *God's* view of your children. You can remind them that they are fearfully and wonderfully made (Psalm 139:14) just the way they are. God loves and cares for them just as they are. You can affirm that your children are all uniquely gifted in ways that make them special.

> **Your words of wisdom and truth can become the sunshine that brightens an otherwise dreary day.**

Such words can heal hearts that hurt and make the everyday problems of life more bearable. God's Word, shared out of your heart, can serve as the one bright star in an otherwise dark sky. Your words of wisdom and truth can become the sunshine that brightens an otherwise dreary day. Your encouragement will supply strength not just for today, but for all your children's tomorrows as well.

Maybe you're thinking of excuses for why you cannot start the day with words of encouragement for your family. Or perhaps you're saying, "I can't be this kind of a dad. I leave for work before my kids

are awake. In fact, I get up before my wife. So I can't encourage anyone at the beginning of the day."

Even if you feel awkward about offering encouragement to your
family, I hope by now you see what a big difference it can make in
the lives of your wife and children when you take time to demonstrate your care for them. Your family really needs you! So if you
have a heavy schedule or find it difficult to talk to your family before
you leave for work, then you need to get creative. For example, you
can leave a note to encourage them as they take that test, apply for
a part-time job, give a verbal report, or whatever. Just the fact that
you are aware of what's happening in their life will be a tremendous
encouragement.

Your kids know how busy you are, and how hard you work. So a
written note from you will serve as a powerful reminder to them that
you love them and are thinking about and praying for them throughout the day. What a dad!

You Can Do It, Dad!

Your background can either be a blessing or a curse. If you came
from a home where encouragement flowed freely, then you may be
saying, "What's the big deal? Why is this guy going on and on about
something that so easy to do?"

If that's the case, then you are truly blessed. But most men are
not so blessed. Many came from homes in which encouragement
was seldom given. They grew up hungering for positive feedback and
instead, they heard words expressing disappointment. And if you
are one of these men, you are probably modeling the way you were
raised. Remember Bill's observation about his soccer kids? "Many
of the parents of these kids express disappointment when their children don't exhibit strong athletic potential. Unfortunately, these parents don't realize the value of encouragement."

Search your heart, Dad. Your kids need all the encouragement
they can get—especially from you, their dad…their hero.

Small Steps That Make a Big Difference

1. *Start out each day by giving encouragement* to your children before you leave for work. If you must depart before they are awake, text them during the day or leave a note in their backpack or lunch bag. And don't forget your wife as you hand out words or notes of encouragement. Include her, and she'll be your best friend forever!

2. *Evaluate your expectations.* Are you trying to relive your life through your children? Is your praise or lack of it based on your expectations, or on their abilities or lack of abilities? Each child is different, and each child isn't you. So you must treat each one as unique and give praise based on their individual efforts and progress. It's not wrong for you to encourage your children to do better, but first praise them for what they have already accomplished.

3. *Begin the day with your Bible in hand.* Remember that a key mark of a dad after God's own heart is that he walks by the Spirit. That requires you to infuse yourself with God's Word so you can draw upon it all day long. Do this in the morning so that when you first greet each member of the family, you'll have the power of the Spirit helping you to be a positive influence on everyone.

4. *Pray for your children.* The best way to encourage your children is to let them know you are praying for them. If you don't already have a prayer notebook, start one now, and set aside a page for each member of your family. On that page, write down the issues your children are facing. What a confidence builder it is for children to know that their dad is praying for them today, and for the rest of their todays!

Encouragement is awesome.
It [can] actually change the course
of another person's day, week, or life. [2]
CHARLES R. SWINDOLL

Coming together is a beginning.
Keeping together is progress.
Working together is success.[1]

HENRY FORD

12

A Dad Who Is a Team Player

Two are better than one,
because they have a good reward for their labor.
For if they fall, one will lift up his companion.

ECCLESIASTES 4:9-10

Greg knocked on the kitchen door, and Bill beckoned for him in enter the house and escape the early morning rain. For nearly a year they had met on Tuesday mornings before work, and Greg looked forward to these times together. Usually he arrived feeling cheerful, but this time he slumped into a chair in a way that made his frustration evident.

Immediately he growled, "I can't believe we lost that game!"

The game Greg was referring to was the big Monday Night Football matchup between Bill and Greg's hometown team and the dreaded Dallas Cowboys. Bill had also watched the game and was a little bummed about it himself. But Bill, ever alert, turned the moment into a discipleship lesson. He asked Greg, "Do you know why our team lost that game?"

"Dallas got lucky!" Greg exclaimed.

"Yes, they did," Bill quickly agreed. "But the real reason we lost is because we didn't play as a team. Our star players tried to win the game all by themselves. Even though Dallas wasn't playing all that well, they still worked together as a team. They drew on the best of each man's abilities. The result was a win."

With that as an opener, Bill had Greg open his Bible to Acts 18 so they could talk about a husband and wife who were team players.

Parenting Is Meant to Be a Team Sport

We have come a long way in our study of what it means to be a dad after God's own heart. We've put together a composite of what God's kind of dad looks like. He is one amazing guy! And, if I'm not mistaken, he looks and acts a lot like you. Like Greg in our chapter-opening stories, you've come a long way in your desire to be God's kind of dad. The infusion of God's Word and your obedience to it are having a powerful and life-changing effect on you. So thanks for hanging in there with me as we've considered the roles and responsibilities God has given to dads.

In this chapter, there is one more role I'd like to discuss with you. It's the role of you working together with your wife as a team as you love and serve God and raise your children to love and serve Him. Right now I want to focus on the *team* aspect in marriage as we look at Aquila and Priscilla, a great couple we meet in the New Testament book of Acts. But first, let's consider a word from the wisest man in the Old Testament, King Solomon.

Two Are Better Than One

King Solomon didn't always live out his wise counsel to others, but his God-breathed wisdom, which is recorded for us in Scripture, can still serve as useful direction for our lives. In Ecclesiastes 4, Solomon recounted the woes and emptiness of the person who is alone, who is without companionship (verse 8). He then says it doesn't have to be that way: "Two are better than one, because they have a good reward for their labor. For if they fall, one will lift up his companion" (Ecclesiastes 4:9-10).

So far this book has purposefully focused on you as a dad and your duties as the point man in the raising of your children. This is biblical. You, as the leader of your family, are the one responsible to God for the raising of your children.

If you are a single dad, this chapter may be a little awkward for you to read. But take heart—there are people in your church who can come alongside you and become a part of your "team." For example, your team could consist of AWANA or Bible club leaders, Sunday school teachers, youth leaders, even other single parents who can work with you as you raise your children.

And if you are married, you are fortunate that God has provided you with a companion—a helper (Genesis 2:18)—who can assist you in the responsibility of raising the children.

Regardless of whether you are married or single, you know you are called to lead, right? And if you are married, the question you need to ask is this: How can I work with my wife as a team to raise our children? Solomon says being a team is productive because "two are better than one" (Ecclesiastes 4:9).

> Before you and your wife can work as a team raising your children, you must first work as a team in your marriage.

Before you and your wife can work as a team raising your children, you must first work as a team in your marriage. Let's look at an amazing couple in the Bible who did just that—Aquila and his wife Priscilla.

The Dynamic Duo

Aquila and Priscilla were a phenomenal couple, truly a couple after God's own heart. Even though they didn't have children, they present a model of how effective you and your wife can be by working together—whether it comes to raising your children, working in your church, or living as a positive Christian influence in your community.

Nothing but positive comments are made about this husband-wife team. Everywhere they lived and ministered, they were blessed and a blessing to both Christians and non-Christians. Here are some highlights of their story:

Aquila and Priscilla helped establish many churches. This couple ministered alongside the apostle Paul while he preached the gospel. Their ministry began in Corinth, where they met Paul. Later, when Paul left Corinth to travel to Ephesus, Priscilla and Aquila went with him (Acts 18:18). We see this dynamic duo assisting Paul and churches in Corinth, Ephesus, and Rome.

Aquila and Priscilla opened their home to believers. When Paul wrote 1 Corinthians, he sent a greeting from this couple, stating, "Aquila and Priscilla greet you heartily in the Lord, with the church that is in their house" (1 Corinthians 16:19).

Aquila and Priscilla earned the apostle Paul's praise. When Paul wrote the book of Romans, he ended his epistle with a greeting to Priscilla and Aquila and praise for them: "Greet Priscilla and Aquila, my fellow workers in Christ Jesus, who risked their own necks for my life, to whom not only I give thanks, but also all the churches of the Gentiles. Likewise greet the church that is in their house" (Romans 16:3-5).

It's obvious this couple made a powerful contribution during the formative years of the church! What were their unique qualifications? Surely they had lots of theological training, right? No. The Bible doesn't say anything about their education. All we know is that they were simple working people—they were tent makers. Nothing special.

So how was God able to use Priscilla and Aquila in such a remarkable way? Together they followed after God's own heart... and they were available! The result? God used them mightily. They were truly a sold-out couple for Christ. And they have much to teach you and your wife about the power of team effort.

The Power of Team Effort

Aquila and Priscilla used their spiritual gifts in complete harmony. It's interesting to note they are never mentioned separately. They worked as a team. And the same could and should be true of you and your wife. When it comes to service and the use of spiritual gifts, each believer is responsible for the development and use of his or her own spiritual gifts. But, as in the case of Aquila and Priscilla, married couples will often find opportunities to work alongside each other in mutual ministry.

When children see their parents working in harmony as a team, it's a picture that is worth a thousand words. A family is a God-ordained institution that brings honor to the Lord as it functions in harmonious unity before a watching world.

Aquila and Priscilla exhibited their faith without competition. You might say this couple was "home schooled." They were fortunate to have the apostle Paul, the writer of 13 books of the New Testament, as their resident teacher while they were in Corinth. Can you imagine the lively discussions they had each day as they sat side by side with Paul while stitching tents? After months or even years of such daily training, they developed an excellent understanding of God's truth and the gospel message.

What's refreshing about this couple is their lack of a competitive spirit when it came to spiritual things. They were both growing spiritually and both serving and ministering. They seemed to have developed a tag-team approach to serving God and His people. You and your wife should take a page out of their playbook and make sure you are both growing spiritually. Then watch how effective the two of you can be as a team.

Dad, be aware that modeling is a mighty molder of hearts and minds. There is no better way to teach your children about mutual love without competition than to let them see it practiced by you and your wife.

Aquila and Priscilla were of one mind regarding hospitality. Aquila and Priscilla did something any couple can do—they opened their home for church ministry. This was how the early church grew. There were no church buildings. Evangelism occurred as people opened their homes for outreach and church worship.

Dad, there is no better training ground for the faith of your children than participating as a family in ministry right in your very own home!

Aquila and Priscilla were both willing to sacrifice. At the end of the book of Romans, Paul sent a special greeting and a few personal comments to his friends about Aquila and Priscilla. Note these final words about them as a couple:

— "Greet Priscilla and Aquila"—They served together.

— "my fellow workers in Christ Jesus"—They served together in the gospel of Christ right alongside Paul.

— "who risked their own necks for my life"—They were both willing to die for the gospel.

—"to whom not only I give thanks"—Paul was thankful
for their many sacrifices.

—"but also all the churches of the Gentiles"—The newly
founded churches were also thankful for this couple's
service and sacrifices (Romans 16:3-4).

Aquila and Priscilla, an amazing couple for Christ, a dynamic
duo, were effective in their service because of their commitment to
their Savior and the grace He extended to them. They were willing
to suffer, and therefore, they were unrestricted. They gave their all,
and God used them mightily.

Dad, how willing are you and your wife to sacrifice not only for
the Lord's service, but also to be stewards of the children the Lord
has given to you? Raising children demands a lifetime of sacrifices.
You may already be in the midst of sacrificing for your kids—money
for medical and dental care, tuition fees for a Christian school education, maybe even more money as Mom stays home instead of
holding down a job. The apostle Paul called all Christians to "present your bodies a living sacrifice" (Romans 12:1). This applies to serving God in every way, including in your role as a parent.

Working as a Team with Your Children

Because all humans are sinners, we are selfish and teamwork does
not come naturally for us. We are individuals with a mind and a will
of our own. We want what we want, even at the cost of others. That's
one reason marriages, especially in the early years, are often rocky.
Each person wants to do things his or her way. It's not until both
husband and wife work things out together, with lots of give-and-
take, that a marriage starts running a lot smoother.

And then when children come along, the dynamic is changed.
And is it ever changed! Suddenly you've added more selfish people
to the mix. So how can you work as a team with this new dynamic,
with you, Dad, as the team leader, and your wife as your co-leader
and helper? Here are a few suggestions for ways the two of you can
work together.

Praying together—What do many football teams do before the start of their next play? They huddle together to talk strategy. Prayer is your "couple huddle." You and your wife bow down together, pray together, and ask God for His wisdom and guidance on the next "play" He wants the two of you to "run" with an ever-changing family. As you pray, you will get to hear what is on each other's hearts. Your wife's concerns for the kids will become your concerns and vice versa, further molding you together as a team.

Planning together—Your team needs to have common goals and direction. Planning together about how to raise your family will give you focus. It will put the two of you on the same page as you agree on a plan and principles for your family. You'll have a foundation for making key decisions. For example, what kind of schooling will you choose—a Christian school, a public school, or home schooling? What kinds of discipline will you use in training your children? As you pool your energies and efforts and create your plans as a couple, you will be working together, and not against each other.

Talking together—Communication is a key factor in every marriage, and also a key to working together in raising the kids. Planning together means you are talking with each other. And when you talk, there are fewer misunderstandings or missed communications. You plan, and then you work the plan—all of which is made possible because you are talking to each other.

Dad, you need to be proactive if there is going to be free-flowing communication between you and your wife. Your input is needed, and you need to find out what your wife is thinking as well. You both need to discuss your options. Then when a problem comes up, you'll already have a plan in place so that it's not a problem after all! All your crises can be solved (or at least kept to a minimum) when the two of you are communicating. Any child-raising issue can be tackled together and resolved.

Serving together—I'm not referring here to ministering as a couple, but to the importance of including your children in ministry projects with you. Work together as a family in your church by participating in projects together. You can minister together at home by hosting an open house at Christmas as a neighborhood outreach. A family that serves together will bond together. As your children see you living out your faith, they will see Christianity not as some theoretical exercise, but as a living reality.

> A family that serves together will bond together.

Having fun together—You and your wife will need to work at balancing out the teaching, training, and discipline with time for good old-fashioned fun with the kids. Go on outings to museums. Travel to state and national parks and historic sites. Set up game nights. Begin the tradition of having "backward dinners," in which you start the meal by eating dessert first. (You can see why backward dinners have always been a favorite at our two daughters' homes!)

Working together—How do you teach your children the importance of doing their work, and doing it in a way that honors the Lord? It starts in the home with you and your wife assigning chores to your children. Even from an early age, children should be taught to pick up their toys, clean their room, and help out with the laundry. Give your kids age-appropriate responsibilities in the yard and the garage. Include your children in the projects you and your wife do around the house. Don't let your children be spectators—figure out how they can help so they can learn how to be responsible for themselves.

Earlier in this book, in the chapter on training, we noted that training is the application of knowledge. You're probably familiar with the following axiom, which I've modified a bit: "Give a child a fish and he can live for a day, but teach a child to fish and he can live for a lifetime." I'm sure some of the skills you have now were learned from your dad when you were younger. I continue to be grateful that my dad taught me how to fix just about everything around the house. Do the same favor for your children!

Have devotions together—This is a common problem area for most families. Why? The family members are rarely all home together at the same time. Dad leaves early or works late. Mom has a job or volunteers her help in the community. The kids have after-school activities and sports practices and games. While such family activity is fairly normal, still, it's vital that you, as the leader of your home, set aside a few minutes each day when everyone can sit at the dining table or in the living room and have a short devotional time. Ideally, you'll want time not just to read from the Bible or a good book, but also to discuss what you've learned. And be sure to pray for each person's day. This exercise teaches volumes to the kids about how important God's Word is to you and Mom. Having a time for devotions also demonstrates that the truth of Scripture can be applied to your children's everyday lives as they step out the front door and into the world.

You Can Do It, Dad!

An unfortunate trend these days is that many dads are giving over the responsibility of parenting to their wives. Rather than doing the "heavy lifting" of parenting, dads are "checking out" and moms are finding themselves having to shoulder the burden of teaching, training, and disciplining alone. Some dads are always gone from home for whatever reason, and others are there, but "not there." They don't get involved with anything having to do with the home or children. They act as though bringing home a paycheck is all that's necessary for fulfilling their God-given responsibility as a parent.

I hope you have determined that will not be true of you. You want to be a good dad—a *great* dad!—and take ownership of your roles and responsibilities. In this book, you've learned what it takes to be a dad after God's own heart. And you've learned that yours is an ongoing responsibility. It won't end when you finish reading this book. You can come back to it again to refresh your commitment, and in the back of this book I've listed additional resources that will help you continue to move toward fulfilling your desire to be a godly dad.

So now, having assumed your role as leader, you can enlist your wife's help. You are ready to lead in the area of raising up your children, and you know that to have the greatest impact, you will need your wife's assistance. Praise God for godly moms who are waiting for godly dads to join forces with them in the training up of the next generation of godly children!

Small Steps That Make a Big Difference

1. *Read books on marriage.* To ensure that your teamwork as a couple stays fresh and vibrant, continue to work on your marriage by reading books on marriage together. A strong marriage will ensure a strong family and provide a great training ground for your children, who will see firsthand what it takes to enjoy a good marriage.

2. *Involve your children in family decisions.* Obviously you and your wife will want to use discretion here, but including your kids in a limited way with helping to make family decisions will create a sense of unity and ownership among them. This will help them to think beyond themselves. (For example, what if you have to change jobs and move to another state? That should create lots of discussion opportunities for you as a family!)

3. *Ask your children to help with vacation planning.* Doing this will help make each member of your family feel more like part of a team. Ask each person what kind of a vacation he or she would enjoy. Camping? Disney World? Winter activities? Obviously, you will want to set some boundaries and a budget. But let each family member dream, speak up, and add their suggestions to the family list. Once you decide on a destination, let the gang help you fill in the details. This will make it their vacation too! Planning together makes for a win-win situation. And a big bonus is that ownership of the vacation will definitely cut down the amount of whining over things the kids didn't get to do.

4. *Stick with the basics.* A dad after God's own heart is a dynamic role. The role of father is constantly changing, shifting, and requiring adjustments on your part as your family grows and changes. You age. Your children age. Friends, activities, and jobs begin to take up more of your children's time. If a family member develops a medical condition, things change.

What can you do to maintain stability in the midst of change? Stick with the basics. Always go back to the basics—God's basics. This book has been about the basics of being a dad, and when your family dynamic changes, do what you've been learning in this book. Keep on doing what you know is right, what you know works. Make the necessary adjustments, seek help if you need it, but don't compromise the basics.

God is the leader of your team.
As you follow Him with all your heart,
you will be leading your team in Jesus' steps.

Jim George

Qualities to Pass On to Your Children

Determination: "Stick with it, regardless."
Honesty: "Speak and live the truth—always."
Responsibility: "Be dependable, be trustworthy."
Thoughtfulness: "Think of others before yourself."
Confidentiality: "Don't tell secrets. Seal your lips."
Punctuality: "Be on time."
Self-Control: "When under stress, stay calm."
Patience: "Fight irritability. Be willing to wait."
Purity: "Reject anything that lowers your standards."
Compassion: "When another hurts, feel it with him."
Diligence: "Work hard. Tough it out."[1]

CHARLES R. SWINDOLL

13

A Dad Who Goes the Distance

Do you not know that in a race all the runners run,
but only one gets the prize?
Run in such a way as to get the prize…
Therefore I do not run like someone running aimlessly.

1 CORINTHIANS 9:24-26 (NIV)

When I was in high school, I tried out for the football team, but that only lasted until I realized I had become the blocking dummy. Next was basketball…but I was too short and a lousy shot, so that was out. That left track and field. I couldn't run very fast, so the sprints weren't an option. I personally ruled out field events like pole vaulting and the long jump…leaving only the distance races. I wasn't particularly good at distance running, but I was the best my small school had to offer!

Well, in the end, I was good enough to get my letter jacket, which, as a teenager, was all I ever really wanted. Wearing that jacket made me a bona fide jock! My track team did manage to win several conference and regional championships, and I even went to the state finals in the half-mile and mile categories before hanging up my running shoes.

Ten years later, I started running again, and have been running three to five times a week ever since. This brings me to the next important quality of a dad after God's own heart: He goes the distance.

Being a Dad Demands Endurance

The race you run as a parent is not a sprint of a few hundred feet at full-out maximum effort…and then it's all over. No, being a dad after God's own heart involves steadily running along day after day—for a lifetime. Being a good dad is like running in a long-distance race. In fact, it's like running a marathon, which is 26 miles and 385 yards, or 42.195 kilometers. To be a marathon dad requires endurance.

I loved watching the sprint races while in high school and continue to enjoy watching them on TV during the Olympics. The sprinters are poised in the blocks. The gun goes off, and in mere seconds, the race is over. Unfortunately some dads see their parenting much the same way. They bring the little one home from the hospital, maybe change a few diapers. They occasionally acknowledge their child's presence. They give a rare smile of approval, or get angry and yell when the child gets on their nerves. But the interaction rarely goes beyond that. It's as if the dad has checked out mentally, and maybe even physically.

Now it's true that many dads have demanding jobs. They leave for work before dawn and don't get home until after dark. For some, it's a dog-eat-dog world in the workplace. The stress and pressure are exhausting, which means they are tired by the time they get home. Some of these dads realize they're not as available to their family as they should be. They often feel like the proverbial hamster on a wheel, trapped in an unrelenting job and unable to get off so they can spend more time with their family. This is a common problem, and these dads know it.

Your solution is to accept the given—you have a job. But you must also accept another given—you are a dad, and as a dad, God has a job for you too. He is asking you to fulfill His will when it comes to the care of your children.

Ask any dad who is trying to be a good dad to compare the demands of his job with those of trying to be a faithful dad. You already know what his answer will be: Hands down, he will tell you being a dad is the most challenging occupation of all. It's a 24/7/365 job when done right. Being a father starts before a child is born and continues until that relationship ceases through death. A dad's duties never end, and never let up. Being a dad after God's own heart demands your *A* game, your best effort, your constant attention, your unrelenting endurance.

So how can you make sure you run the fathering race with endurance? How can you keep from giving in or giving up, especially during the difficult times?

Here are some coaching tips for you as you train for the marathon of being a dad after God's own heart:

Being a Dad Requires Oversight

Oversight refers to stewardship. In Bible times, a steward was put in charge of his master's possessions. He was accountable for both profit and loss. He was...

> ...*a guardian* in whose care possessions were entrusted. He would willingly sacrifice himself to keep his master's goods safe.

> ...*a manager* who had been given a responsibility. He was to supervise his master's household, oversee the servants, dispense resources, and handle business and financial affairs.

The apostle Paul saw his call to ministry as a stewardship entrusted to him from the Lord. The church is God's household, and Paul was given the task of leading and caring for the churches under his care. He was accountable to God. This is how Paul described his ministry: "I became a minister according to the stewardship from God which was given to me for you, to fulfill the word of God" (Colossians 1:25).

As a dad, you too have been given a stewardship. You are responsible for managing the goods and resources that God has put under your charge. Included in that charge is the care of your children. You are both a guardian and a manager of the spiritual welfare of the children God has entrusted to you.

Jesus felt deeply and strongly about children, and you should too. When the disciples wanted to send the little ones away, Jesus countered their dismissal of the children, saying, "Let the little children come to Me, and do not forbid them; for of such is the kingdom of heaven" (Matthew 19:14).

Being a Dad Requires Balance

A father is to provide for physical needs. You, Dad, are responsible to meet your family's needs, which requires that you work so you can provide for your wife and children. Because work is sometimes hard, we tend to view it as a bad thing. But in the Bible, work is seen as a good, normal, and natural part of a man's daily life. The book of Proverbs has high regard for those who are diligent workers:

> He who tills his land will be satisfied with bread,
> but he who follows frivolity is devoid of understanding
> (12:11).

> In all labor there is profit,
> but idle chatter leads only to poverty (14:23).

> Do you see a man who excels in his work?
> He will stand before kings;
> He will not stand before unknown men (22:29).

In addition to providing for the physical needs of his family, a father also looks after the spiritual and emotional needs of those in his home.

Are you wondering how, as a busy dad, you can take care of all these needs? The bottom line is one of balance. It's being able to balance the demands of your work with having a close relationship with your kids. If your work or the amount of time you spend at work is adversely affecting your relationship with your wife and children, then you need to stop and evaluate your priorities. You need to ask yourself: Where is the balance?

I realize that today's jobs often require a lot of a man's time, even when he is away from work. The technological intrusions of email, instant messaging, fax machines, and digital voice mail make it more difficult to get away from one's job.

But then there are choices we make that can affect the amount of time we as dads spend with our families. For example, we decide to buy a bigger home, better furniture, more playthings for fun and frills. All these choices come at a cost—and usually they mean working harder and longer so we can pay for them. And then there's the choice of working longer hours simply because we prefer to work than to spend time with our families.

Whatever the case, if you've allowed work to become an obsession or a priority at the expense of your family, then you're putting your health and family relationships at risk. No job is worth losing your health or your wife and children. That's why balance is so important.

Take another look at the table of contents at the front of this book. It lists the roles and responsibilities God has called you to fulfill as a dad. Hopefully, this list will inspire you to focus more on your kids. You may be very good at what you do on the job and a hard worker, but in God's eyes, that's a distant second to being a strong dad. I'm praying that, with God's help and by His grace, you will embrace your calling to be a dad after God's own heart.

Being a Dad Requires Discipline

The ancient Greeks observed two great athletic events in the day of the apostle Paul. We all know of the most famous and popular one—the Olympic Games. But there was another event called the Isthmian Games because it was held in Corinth, which was located on a narrow isthmus between the Gulf of Corinth and the Saronic Gulf. Paul saw the idea of running a race as a useful analogy for describing the nature of his service to God. He saw usefulness to God as being in direct proportion to his attitude toward discipline. Note how Paul described his determination to accomplish his goal, which illustrates well the kind of determination you and I need as dads:

> Everyone who competes in the games exercises self-control in all things. They then do it to receive a perishable wreath, but we an imperishable. Therefore I run in such a way, as not without aim; I box in such a way, as not beating the air; but I discipline my body and make it my slave, so that, after I have preached to others, I myself will not be disqualified (1 Corinthians 9:25-27 NASB).

A Dad Must Have Self-Control (verse 25)

Paul saw having "self-control in all things" as a key to his success. In the original Greek text of the New Testament, the term translated "self-control" means "self-restraint" or "rigid self-control." It has the idea of strength under control. A dad must have this quality of self-control. As a man, you have many areas of life in which you can be tempted and succumb to a lack of control:

Sexual area—The world offers husbands and dads daily temptations and opportunities to give in to touching, flirting, even viewing pornography, which can ruin marriage and family relationships and even lead to the ultimate loss of self-control—infidelity. A lack of sexual self-control destroys the bond of love and trust that should exist between a man and his wife and children.

Emotional area—A dad needs to show emotional love and care for his children. Unfortunately, it's all too easy for us to get frustrated with our kids and express the wrong kinds of emotions, such as anger. If you yell at your children or have temper flare-ups, you will end up doing serious damage to your relationships with your children. They will become fearful of you and think of you as a smoldering volcano. They will always be on edge around you because they never know when you're going to erupt.

Physical areas—This can include failing to take care of your health (either through working too hard or laziness), lack of exercise, or poor eating choices. Don't delude yourself by saying you can afford to neglect your health now and do a better job later. We say that we'll start exercising or eating better tomorrow—except that tomorrow never arrives.

You probably know guys who started out taking an occasional business drink yet ending up with a drinking problem. Smoking is another harmful and addictive habit. A lack of self-control when it comes to food, sex, alcohol, tobacco, and even things like golf will make it harder for you to exercise the kind of discipline that will make you a good dad. Remember that your kids are watching you. If you don't practice self-control, they won't have any reason to either.

That's why it's so important for you to constantly, minute-by-minute lean on God's strength and grace and walk by the Spirit. When you involve God in all your choices, you will have the self-control you need.

A Dad Must Have Focus—(verses 25-26)

Paul's focus was on the salvation of the lost (verses 19,22). That was his calling from God and therefore his goal. He did not try to run his race "without aim." Running your race as a dad requires this same intent focus on your goal. Your "aim" is to run alongside your children and do all you can to help them come to salvation in Christ. A dad cannot let anything sidetrack him from this focus.

What do you want as the end product of your parenting? A sports star? A scholar with a 4.0 grade point average? Or do you live to see the salvation of your children? This, my friend, is the goal of a dad after God's own heart, and everything else is secondary to it. This is where your focus must be. Spend every day of your life preparing your children to know God through Jesus Christ and to live their lives after God's own heart.

> **Your "aim" is to run alongside your children and do all you can to help them come to salvation in Christ.**

A Dad Must Follow God's Rules (verse 27)

If a dad doesn't know and follow God's rules for running the race, he can be disqualified (verse 27). In Paul's day, any contestant in the Olympic Games who failed to meet the rules could not participate in the games. You are a dad by virtue of the birth of your child. The issue is, are you going to be a dad after *God's* own heart, or are you going to be a dad after *your* own heart?

A dad disqualifies himself if he is unwilling to pay the price required to be God's kind of dad. Ignorance is no excuse. In a race, being ignorant of the rule that says a runner cannot step outside of his lane does not excuse him from being disqualified. A vital part of participation is knowing the rules and keeping those rules.

The same is true of your parenting. God has established guidelines for fathers, and He expects you to follow them. They are clearly stated in the Bible, and you are to care enough to take the time to know them and follow them.

Want to know what helped to motivate me to be a dad who followed God's rules? The Bible asks, "What will it profit a man if he gains the whole world, and loses his own soul?" (Mark 8:36). As a dad, I have often applied this verse to my parenting by paraphrasing it to read, "What will it profit a dad if he gains the whole world, and loses his own son or daughter?"

Don't drop out of the parenting race. Your children need you— *all* of you. And don't fail to follow God's guidelines for fathers and disqualify yourself. Again, your children need you—all of you, right alongside them, every step of the way.

Being a Dad Requires Effort

Your children only have one dad—you. No matter how they came to be in your family, if they are in your home, they are in your care. No one else can fill a dad's role in your children's lives. By now, after reading this book, I'm sure you are not taking your position as a parent lightly. You are realizing that being God's kind of dad takes effort—lots of effort!

But just like an athlete who has coaches and trainers and equipment to help him perform his very best, you too have help that can keep you on top of your dad-game. God has provided you with some valuable resources that can assist you in fulfilling your stewardship— you are not alone. He has done His part; now it's up to you to do yours.

What are some of the resources God has given you?

The Holy Spirit—The Spirit empowers you through God's Word. When my girls were little toddlers, I purchased a Bible and began to read it each day. God's Spirit started working me over and convicted me that my priorities were all wrong. For the first time I began to realize what it meant to be a father who would "bring [my girls] up in the training and admonition of the Lord" (Ephesians 6:4). If you are a believer in Christ, God has given you this same Bible and this same Spirit. Read your Bible. Follow the guidelines God placed in it. Be God's kind of father to your children.

Godly examples—There are men in your church who are a few steps ahead of you in the fathering race, and there may even be some who are quite far along in the race. God has provided them to give you help. So reach out. Ask for their help, their advice.

Perhaps you could do what Greg and Bill did, and meet once a week. Ask for one of these mature men to meet with you so you can learn from his wisdom and experience. Ask him to go through this book with you and add his input. When my children were growing up, at each stage of their development I would seek out men who had survived that stage and had wisdom to share so I could be a better dad.

This process is called *mentoring*, and the word mentor has an interesting story behind it. According to ancient Greek mythology, a man named Mentor tutored the son of the great warrior Odysseus, who had to leave home to go fight in the Trojan War. After the war, Odysseus was not able to return home for many more years. During all that time, Mentor raised Odysseus's son, Telemachus, and taught and trained him for life. That is what other dads did for me when I was raising my children, and that is what other men can do for you as well. They can mentor you through your dad years and help you fulfill the responsibilities of being a dad.

Christian books—My hat is off to you for reading this book—not because it's a book I wrote, but because it's a book! Not a lot of dads read books, especially books on parenting. In a casual search of Amazon.com, I discovered there are nearly 80,000 books that have more or less to do with the subject of parenting, and you can be certain there are many Christian books included in that number. Books will help supplement what you are learning from your mentors. And if you cannot find a mentor, then the authors of Christian books can become your mentors.

Being a Dad Requires Being a Dad Today

Distance running is as much a mental feat as a physical one. If during the early stages of my daily run I think about how many miles I have left to go, I can quickly feel overwhelmed or defeated.

But when I concentrate on the path directly in front of me and think only about my next step, I find it much easier to keep making progress toward the finish line.

If you were to take a moment right now to start thinking about all that's involved in raising a child after God's own heart—from birth to the time the child leaves home—I guarantee you will be overwhelmed by the magnitude and seriousness of the task. It's very sobering to consider that you have stewardship over a human soul who will live for eternity. That's pretty monumental, isn't it? Yes, it's true that it is God who determines the eternal destiny of your children. But humanly speaking, you and your wife are responsible for their physical, mental, and spiritual development.

So as you focus on your task as a dad after God's own heart, think only about the road directly in front of you—this very day, the day that you are living in right now, the day that's in front of you. Think of the value of just this one day. It consists of 24 hours, or 1440 minutes, or 86,400 seconds. Your motto needs to be *carpe diem*—"Seize the day." You must take hold of just this one day and attempt to do your best—to be the best dad you can be to your children...just for this day. Then wake up tomorrow. Reflect upon yesterday, rejoice in its victories, learn from its defeats, and then, by the grace of God, step out into your new day and try again to be an even better dad just for this one new day.

> One day is all you have at the moment, but eternity is wrapped up in it.

Dad, you know there will be times that you fail. But the secret to long-term success is to not give up. The prize of raising up a child who loves God is too great to give up when adversity comes your way. Make each day count. Live each day as if it's your last day on earth with your children. Plan for it. Cherish it. Welcome it. Evaluate it. Learn from it. And most important of all, enjoy it.

What will happen when you live out your parenting role one day at a time? For sure, you will be enjoying it! You won't be worrying about tomorrow because you are being the best dad you know how to be today. Soon you will begin stringing your good dad-days together. You'll find yourself wanting to freeze-frame each season of your children's lives because you will all be having so much fun at each stage of life.

One day is all you have at the moment, but eternity is wrapped up in it. So cherish today with your children, and do the same again tomorrow. Then one day, with God's help, you will stand with pride and amazement as you walk your beautiful, grown-up daughter down the aisle to the waiting arms of a godly young man—the man you prayed for every day of her life. Or you will be sitting in the audience as your son walks across a stage with his college diploma in hand—a godly son who is ready to brave society as a strong, vibrant Christian.

I'm sure you have dreams and visions of your children's futures. Whether they marry or not, get a college degree or not, is not the point. The point is that your children represent God's next generation. Hopefully they are prepared to live as you have lived—after God's own heart—and then repeat the process with their own children. As a dad who is willing to go the distance, you have a contribution to make. Do as the psalmist did: "I will make Your name to be remembered in all generations; therefore the people shall praise You forever and ever" (Psalm 45:17).

I can't help but end this chapter where I began it—with the illustration of running a marathon. I've been told that the secret to finishing well in a marathon is finding or hitting a "stride"—that is, setting yourself into a pace and rhythm that works. Likewise, when it comes to being a dad after God's own heart and raising children after God's own heart, finding your stride is the secret to doing well. Developing your own dad-rhythm and routine is the key to successful long-distance parenting.

Try to settle into a pace that has as few variables as possible. Above all, make sure God is at the center of everything you do as a family—that you are a family after God's own heart. Then do your part to make your home a happy, peaceful, safe place for your children. And don't be surprised if this wonderful home atmosphere makes their friends want to hang out at your house as well.

So find your stride…and enjoy your run!

You Can Do It, Dad!

You now have a lot of information and responsibilities to think about and pray about. I want to encourage you one last time to take your role as a father seriously. Take time to pause and think about what's involved in being a dad after God's own heart. There is no greater goal than being God's kind of dad. Once you get this goal firmly fixed in your heart and mind, make it a point to remind yourself each morning before you get out of bed: "Today I'm going to be a dad after God's own heart!"

Then, with all the confidence and strength that comes from knowing and acknowledging this part of God's will for your day, leap out of bed with excitement and enthusiasm and go do it!

Small Steps That Make a Big Difference

1. *Evaluate your priorities.* It's easy to think that you are doing what's best for your children by working hard to provide them with stuff, stuff, and more stuff: good schools, private lessons, the latest fashions, the newest smart phone, and, of course, a TV and Internet for their rooms. The list could go on and on. But what your children need most is a dad who has mentally, physically, and spiritually placed himself at the top of their list of essentials—they've got a dad who's fully on board. How does your list of priorities read? Evaluating your priorities is a small but important step to being a better dad.

2. *Evaluate your schedule.* It's also easy to assume your priorities are already in order and that your family comes first. But what you *think* and what you're *really doing* may be very different. But make a list of your commitments, activities, and hobbies. Other than work, what is consuming the majority of your time? What does your schedule reveal about your focus? Who or what is receiving the bulk of your time and attention? If your children are not at the top or near the top or your list, what will it take to make sure you spend more time with your family?

3. *Make some changes.* As you are taking these small steps of evaluating your priorities and schedule, are you shocked by the amount of

time you are spending on the pursuit of things other than being the best dad you can be? If so, start turning things around. Start small. Then, as you begin to see the positive responses in your children, step up your efforts and think about bigger changes you can make.

4. *Start fresh each day.* A dad after God's own heart doesn't rest on yesterday's results. And if yesterday's results weren't so good, don't dwell on them. If they were good, don't use that as an excuse to relax. Start fresh each day with a clean slate of desires, expectations, and dreams for your family and for yourself as a father. What is it you can do today to be the best dad possible, just for today?

5. *Start with one decision that will make a big difference.* If your schedule (or self-centeredness or lack of motivation) is keeping you from being involved in your children's lives, ask God what choices you can make that will give you more hands-on time and interaction with your family. And don't forget to ask your wife for her input. Start with one choice that will involve you with the children. It could be as small and easy as helping the kids get ready for school.

6. *Make a decision to demonstrate your love.* All the "small steps" mentioned above will show your children that you love and care about them. But it's also important that you verbalize your love. You cannot say "I love you" enough, and you cannot demonstrate your love enough. No child has ever been adversely affected by an overdose of love.

Dad, your guiding hand on my shoulder
will remain with me forever.
AUTHOR UNKNOWN

STUDY GUIDE

A Dad Who Has a Divine Model

1. Every dad needs help. And every dad needs a model. Think about the men in your church. Is there one you might approach for help and advice and maybe even a mentoring relationship? Jot down some names and start praying.

2. God is the ultimate and perfect model of fatherhood. What aspects of His role as Father do you see in the following verses?

Psalm 68:5—

Psalm 89:26—

Psalm 103:13—

3. Look at Romans 4:11 in your Bible and scan through the section "The Father of Those Who Believe." What does "Father of those who believe" mean to you personally? (If you are unsure how to answer this question, be sure and ask one of the men you identified in Question 1, or ask your pastor to explain this to you.)

4. In your Bible, read 1 Samuel 2:12-25. What did Eli's sons do that was wrong or evil?

What did Eli do that was wrong or evil?

In the section entitled "You Can Do It, Dad!" you read this statement: "Your children are yours to influence for good or evil." How did Eli live out this statement as a father?

5. Choose one of the "Small Steps That Make a Big Difference" and commit to working on it this week. Write it out here, along with some actions you will take right away.

6. What one truth from this chapter had the greatest impact on you as a dad, and why?

(2)

A Dad Who Walks in the Spirit

1. Read Galatians 5:22-23 in your Bible and list the fruit of the Spirit here. Why you think these qualities would be important for you to show as a dad?

2. Quickly review the section under each of the nine fruit of the Spirit. Which two sections—or fruit—spoke to you about actions or attitudes you are exhibiting toward your children that need to be corrected? Write out a plan for beginning to make changes in each one.

—

—

3. If a person asked you to explain what it means to "walk in the Spirit," what would you say? (Hint: See the explanation in the section "The Art of Walking.")

4. Look again at the section entitled "The Art of Walking." Then, in a few words, write out what it means to "abide in Christ."

5. Continuing on with "The Art of Walking," list the four "choices" you can make that will keep you close to Jesus.

—

—

—

—

As you think about and look at your daily life and routine, what changes can you make that will promote your spiritual growth and enhance your walk with Christ…and when do you plan to make them?

6. Choose one of the "Small Steps that Make a Big Difference" and commit to working on it this week. Write it out here, along with some actions you will take right away.

7. What one truth from this chapter had the greatest impact on you as a dad, and why?

A Dad Who Is a Teacher

1. Look at Deuteronomy 6:6-7 in your Bible. What parenting instructions does God give parents in...

Verse 6—

Verse 7—

Why are these verses important to you as a dad?

2. According to Deuteronomy 6:5, what is your first priority as a parent?

3. Read the verses below in your Bible and note what each one tells you about how to internalize God's Word.

Joshua 1:8—

Psalm 119:11—

Proverbs 7:1-3—

Colossians 3:16—

How does having God's Word in your heart enhance your role as a teacher to your children?

4. Deuteronomy 6:6-7 commands dads to teach God's Word to their children. What can you do today to improve follow-through on God's command? And how about tomorrow?

5. Write out the four key opportunities you have every day to teach your children about God by "talking" to them.

—

—

—

—

To do what God is asking, what is required of you? (List several choices you must make each day.)

6. Choose one of the "Small Steps That Make a Big Difference" and commit to working on it this week. Write it out here, along with some actions you will take right away.

7. What one truth from this chapter had the greatest impact on you as a dad, and why?

A Dad Who Is a Trainer

1. Read again the opening story. Can you relate to Greg's unsettled concern about teaching and training his children? What are some of your concerns about your teaching role in your children's lives?

2. In a few words, sum up what this chapter highlights as the differences between *teaching* and *training*.

   Teaching my children involves—

   Training my children involves—

3. Training children is a recurring theme in the Bible. What do these verses say about training your children?

   Proverbs 22:6—

   Ephesians 6:4—

2 Timothy 3:14-15—

4. God provides two training grounds for your children—your home and your church. What efforts are you currently making to train your children at home?

If you haven't started your in-home training, what would be a good first step for you—and when will you take that step?

5. God's second training ground for your children is your church. Take another look in this chapter at the list of excuses some dads use for not getting their family to church. Which excuses have you used—or been tempted to use—at times?

What does Hebrews 10:24-25 communicate about God's desire for His people to come together for worship?

6. Read Luke 2:41-49. What does this scene reveal about Jesus' parents' commitment to fulfill God's commands that His people gather to worship Him?

In Jesus' life as a 12-year-old, how important was this journey so His family could worship God? What happened while Jesus was there?

Obviously Jesus' parents were committed to worship in the way God prescribed. And obviously they were committed to taking Jesus with them. One scholar made this comment about Jesus' parents:

> Jesus' family had the right priorities. Families that establish regular habits of worship are less likely to have their spiritual life deflected by alternative attractions. Keep worship on top of your family's agenda. Putting God first is a great example to children, who quickly learn what parents care about by observing how they plan and spend time.[1]

How important is regular worship...

to your spiritual growth?

to your children's spiritual development?

7. Choose one of the "Small Steps That Make a Big Difference" and commit to working on it this week. Write it out here, along with some actions you will take right away.

8. What one truth from this chapter had the greatest impact on you as a dad, and why?

(5)

A Dad Who Is an Instructor

1. The military has certain objectives for its recruits. In your role of "drill instructor," what is your primary objective as outlined in the section entitled "Taking on Another Mission"?

2. Obedience does not mean perfection. It means a willingness to obey even when confronted with sin. This chapter contrasts the hearts of two men—Saul and David. Read 1 Samuel 15:10-23 and briefly describe how King Saul's actions demonstrated a disobedient heart.

Now read 2 Samuel 12:1-13 and briefly describe how David's responses to God's rebuke through the prophet Nathan revealed an obedient heart.

3. Scan the section entitled "Successful Training Starts with You." What is the bottom-line message to you as a dad?

4. As you think about the "10 Reasons Dads Don't Discipline," list the three reasons that you struggle with the most, and why:

—

—

—

How have your views changed since starting to read this book, and what are you doing about it?

5. Choose one of the "Small Steps That Make a Big Difference" and commit to working on it this week. Write it out here, along with some actions you will take right away.

6. What one truth from this chapter had the greatest impact on you as a dad, and why?

A Dad Who Is an Intercessor

1. Here's something for you to think about: Why is being an intercessor for your children the easiest role for a dad to attempt, but the hardest to faithfully practice day after day, year after year?

2. Read Job 1:1-5 and list Job's concerns for his children. What did he do about his concerns?

What message is Job's example sending to you as a father?

3. Read Genesis 18:20-33. Keep in mind that Abraham's nephew Lot and his family are living in Sodom and Gomorrah. This passage in the Bible is considered to be a classic example of intercessory prayer. From Abraham's dialogue with God, what do you learn about God?

What do you learn from Abraham about intercessory prayer?

PS: See Genesis 19:29 for the outcome of Abraham's intercession. What happened?

Bonus Questions: Read 2 Samuel 12:13-23. This passage looks at what happened after David's sin with Bathsheba, who was another man's wife, and after Nathan, the prophet, confronted David regarding his sin and the consequences—his son would die. How did David respond to the child's sickness in verses 16-17?

How long did David continue to intercede on behalf of his son (verse 18)?

What do you learn about intercessory prayer on behalf of your children from David's example?

4. Skim through the section "Understanding Prayer" and write down one concept about prayer that was new to you or served as a good reminder. Why did you select this particular concept?

5. Scan through the section "The Problem of Praying" and record the one reason you most identify with.

What first step can you take to start praying more—and when?

6. Choose one of the "Small Steps That Make a Big Difference" and commit to working on it this week. Write it out here, along with some actions you will take right away.

7. What one truth from this chapter had the greatest impact on you as a dad, and why?

A Dad Who Is a Prayer Warrior

1. Glance through the opening story of this chapter and note Bill's statement, "Intercession is reactive…, but being a prayer warrior is proactive." The previous chapter was about intercession—praying on behalf of your loved ones. How do you see being a prayer warrior as proactive?

2. Read Ephesians 6:10-17 in your Bible. What makes these verses especially helpful for you as a dad who is to be a prayer warrior for his family?

3. Ephesians 6:18 gives you your "marching orders" as a prayer warrior. What does verse 18 say about:

The frequency of your prayers?

The variety of your prayers?

The force of your prayers?

The attitude of your prayers?

The resolve of your prayers?

The objects of your prayers?

4. From the section entitled "What Is Required to Be a Prayer Warrior?" list the two requirements. Then describe why each one is important for being a dad who battles for his children in prayer.

First...

Because...

Second...

Because...

5. The apostle Paul was a mighty prayer warrior and shows you how to be proactive through prayer for your children. Take a few minutes and note the content of Paul's prayers for his "children" in the faith in these verses:

Romans 1:9-10—

Philippians 1:4,9-11—

Colossians 1:3,9-11—

2 Thessalonians 1:11—

2 Timothy 1:3—

Philemon 4—

Paul prayed specifically for his children in the faith, and you can—and should—too. To begin walking the path of a prayer warrior, determine one "specific" you need to pray for concerning each of your children. Write the specific(s) here, and let the battle begin!

6. Choose one of the "Small Steps That Make a Big Difference" and commit to working on it this week. Write it out here, along with some actions you will take right away.

7. What one truth from this chapter had the greatest impact on you as a dad, and why?

(8)

A Dad Who Is a Shepherd

1. What does a shepherd do? Look at these verses in your Bible. In a few words, describe the activities of a shepherd.

Genesis 31:40: A shepherd _____

1 Samuel 17:34-36: A shepherd _____

Psalm 23:1: A shepherd _____

John 10:11: A shepherd _____

John 10:14: A shepherd _____

How are you doing in the shepherding department, Dad? Check the one that needs your immediate attention the most, write out what you plan to do, and tackle it today. Your sheep will appreciate it!

2. Look again at the section "A Dad Feeds His Flock" and compare what you are already doing with what is listed as suggestions. What other activities would you like to also implement from this section?

Can you think of other practices you could try that would center your children's lives around God's Word? Jot them down and pray about them.

3. A shepherd leads his flock—and so does a dad. Comment on each of these statements as it applies to leading your family:

Leadership is a lifestyle—You can't turn it on and off. How can you be more consistent in your leadership at home?

Leadership allows for help—You can partner with your wife, with grandparents, with your children's teachers, and with your church leaders. Who's on your leadership team?

Leadership takes an interest—Sheep thrive on personal attention and time with their shepherd, and it's no different for your children. How interested are you in your flock? How—and when—can you spend more time each day with each child?

Leadership seeks advice—You can and should seek advice as a dad from dads who have gone before you. By seeking wise counsel, you can cut down on the number of mistakes you make. Who makes up your corps of counselors?

Leadership follows the manual—Do you want fewer problems for you and your family? Do you need answers and solutions to the problems you do have? Then read and follow the ultimate manual, the Bible. If you don't know where to start, read the book of Joshua or the book of Nehemiah to see leaders in action and the qualities that made them leaders.

4. Choose one of the "Small Steps That Make a Big Difference" and commit to working on it this week. Write it out here, along with some actions you will take right away.

5. What one truth from this chapter had the greatest impact on you as a dad, and why?

A Dad Who Is a Watchman

1. Read Acts 20:29-31 in your Bible and describe why the apostle Paul wanted those in leadership to be vigilant in their watch-care over the people in the church.

What similarities are there between Paul's concern for the spiritual condition and safety of the church and your concern for your own family's spiritual condition and safety?

2. In the section entitled "The Role of a Watchman," what two ways are suggested for keeping yourself vigilant as a watchman?

—

—

Jot down what you are currently doing—or need to be doing—to keep sharp in your vigilance as you watch over your family.

3. Watching is one aspect of your duties as a dad. What is your other duty and responsibility as a dad when you see the enemy approaching?

Take a few minutes to think about each one of your children. What areas of concern are you seeing in each of their lives right now? What do you, the watchman of your family, need to do immediately to warn your children, even if you are sure to be seen as the "bad guy"?

4. The analogy of moving a football (a child) down the field toward the goal line is a good way to measure your involvement and commitment to raising your children to become men and women after God's own heart. Where do you see your commitment level on the 100-yard playing field? As a watchman, do you need to speak up more? To be more involved? To go shoulder-to-shoulder with your child?

Take a few minutes to honestly assess the level of your desire to be a committed, all-the-way-to-the-end watchman. Jot down some "Notes to Self" to help you with your plan to be more involved as a dad.

5. Choose one of the "Small Steps That Make a Big Difference" and commit to working on it this week. Write it out here, along with some actions you will take right away.

6. What one truth from this chapter had the greatest impact on you as a dad, and why?

A Dad Who Is a Guide

1. According to the following verses, what is God's Word telling you about some of God's purposes for you as a dad?

Deuteronomy 6:6-7—

Proverbs 22:6—

Ephesians 6:4—

How should knowing these specific purposes for you as a father impact or dictate your priorities?

A problem defined is a problem half-solved. What changes or adjustments do you need to make to your priorities so you can better live out God's purposes?

2. As a dad, you are also tasked by God to guide your children toward finding God's purpose. Write out the five lifelong practices that will give your children direction. Because a guide leads the way, state how you will model these practices for your children. Be specific.

Practice #1—

How will you specifically model this?

Practice #2—

How will you specifically model this?

Practice #3—

How will you specifically model this?

Practice #4—

How will you specifically model this?

Practice #5—

How will you specifically model this?

3. "Seeking the Higher Road" (Practice #5) is a rarity in the world. Take a minute or two to reflect on this concept by writing out three verses from your Bible:

Ecclesiastes 9:10—

1 Corinthians 10:31—

Colossians 3:23-24—

How important to you is honoring God? How often do you think about it, seek it, aim for it? With pen in hand, write out today's date and your personal commitment to begin to stop, think, pray, and seek the higher road of excellence in all your choices—to purposefully choose to walk the road that will bring glory to God.

Today's date: _____

My commitment:

4. Choose one of the "Small Steps That Make a Big Difference" and commit to working on it this week. Write it out here, along with some actions you will take right away.

5. What one truth from this chapter had the greatest impact on you as a dad, and why?

(11)

A Dad Who Is an Encourager

1. Glance back through Bill and Greg's conversation at soccer practice. Think about Bill's words: "Many of the parents of these kids express disappointment when their children don't exhibit strong athletic potential. Unfortunately, these parents don't realize the value of encouragement."

Now think about this past week. Can you pinpoint any specific times you gave a word of encouragement to each of your children? What happened? What was your child's reaction or response?

If you are having trouble thinking of a time, then this chapter should speak to you. Like Bill told Greg, "Don't be a dad who sees only what your daughter can't do, but see what she can do. Be your daughter's biggest fan!"

2. Read John 16:32-33. In this passage, Jesus recognized His disciples' distress and encouraged them. We see and hear Jesus laying a solid foundation for the disciples' courage and confidence in the face trials and tribulation. Write out the portions of verse 33 that show that Jesus...

told them the truth—

gave them comfort—

gave them a reason to be confident and courageous—

What do you learn from Jesus' interaction with His disciples about encouraging your children? Or put another way, what will you do or do differently the next time you sense distress in your children? What do you want to remember to do—and not do?

3. In the section entitled "How to Be Your Children's #1 Encourager," what is stated as the #1 rule you must follow, and why do you think this is important?

4. According to "How to Be Your Children's #1 Encourager," you need to make three decisions. Write them here and describe how each of these decisions can ensure your encouragement is authentic and your excitement is genuine.

Decision #1—

Decision #2—

Decision #3—

5. Choose one of the "Small Steps That Make a Big Difference" and commit to working on it this week. Write it out here, along with some actions you will take right away.

6. What one truth from this chapter had the greatest impact on you as a dad, and why?

A Dad Who Is a Team Player

Dad, as you begin to answer these questions, why not invite your wife to go through this chapter with you? Then you can answer these questions together—as a team.

1. In Ecclesiastes 4:9, King Solomon wrote, "Two are better than one." With Solomon's words in mind, look at Deuteronomy 6:6-7. How can you and your wife act as a team to fulfill God's instructions about teaching your children? List several ways your wife can—or does— help you with this responsibility.

2. Read Genesis 2:18. How did God describe Eve's role as Adam's wife?

The role of "helper" has been defined and explained as one who shares a man's responsibilities, responds to his nature with understanding and love, and wholeheartedly cooperates with him in working out the plan of God.[2] Isn't it thrilling to know that together, you and your wife can work out the plan of God? What a blessing you are to each other. And what a blessing you are to your children. And what a blessing the two of you will share, knowing that, as a team, you are pleasing God by living out His will. Truly, two are better than one!

3. Healthy parenting starts with a healthy marriage. List the four ways Aquila and Priscilla demonstrated "The Power of Team Effort" as a couple.

—

—

—

—

What are some lessons you and your wife can learn from this dynamic couple—lessons that can make your marriage and parenting more effective?

4. List the seven suggestions for "Working as a Team with Your Children."

—

—

—

—

—

—

—

Check the ones you are presently working on together as a couple.

For each item on the list that is without a check mark, write down one step that you and your wife can take, as soon as possible, to put it into action. It won't be long until you are even more productive as a parenting team!

5. Choose one of the "Small Steps That Make a Big Difference" and commit to working on it this week. Write it out here, along with some actions you will take right away.

6. What one truth from this chapter had the greatest impact on you as a dad, and why?

A Dad Who Goes The Distance

1. Can you recall a super-challenging hike, climb, ride, or run that you have experienced? Describe the physical and mental effort it required of you. Share a few highlights (or lowlights!) of that experience here.

Now think about your children and your super-challenging role as a dad. Are you applying and expending the same amount of time and the same kind of energy today on your responsibilities as a father? You already know that raising children who follow God is an effort much grander than completing a trek. It's a responsibility that affects every member of your family and counts for eternity.

2. A dad after God's own heart commits every facet of his life to raising and caring for his children. And he gladly gives 100 percent of his physical and mental efforts to fulfilling God's challenge to endure to the end, to "go the distance" as a dad. What is required to go the distance—to be a dad after God's own heart? Answering the questions that follow will guide you in your quest to go the distance with your kids.

A dad after God's own heart provides oversight. You are the one in charge and accountable to God for your family. What does 1 Corinthians 4:2 say is required of a steward or overseer?

A dad after God's own heart lives a balanced life. What is your greatest struggle in keeping a balance between your roles as a provider and a parent? What changes may be in order?

A dad after God's own heart pays the price to be self-disciplined and self-controlled. In the section entitled "Being a Dad Requires Discipline," three essentials were drawn from 1 Corinthians 9:25-27. With your Bible open to these verses, summarize how each of these essentials applies to you as a dad who desires to go the distance—and win.

Self-control (verse 25)—

Focus (verse 26)—

Following God's "rules" (verse 27)—

Being a dad after God's own heart requires tremendous effort. But be encouraged—you are not alone. As you make your way through the "resource list" below, make a note of how each one of them can assist you in your awesome responsibility of raising children after God's own heart.

Help from God—God Himself, God's Word, and the Holy Spirit are solid resources. Look up these key verses and share briefly how these truths should and can encourage you to go the distance.

Joshua 1:9—

2 Timothy 3:16-17—

2 Peter 1:3-4—

John 16:13—

Help from others—In addition to His help, God has also given you an army of people as resources who can help you go the distance as a dad. Look up the key verses below and share briefly how they should and can encourage you to go the distance.

Help from your spouse—You and your children's mother care more about your family than anyone else in the world. Team up with your wife and present a solid front and an example of a great marriage to your children.

Genesis 2:18—

Help from your church—Being a Christian places you into the family of God. Think of your church body, your church family as filled with people who can partner with you as you parent your children. Among them you will find mentors, counselors, pastors, and maybe even parenting classes and groups.

Hebrews 10:24-25—

Your extended family—Your family is a gift from God. Your parents and grandparents are a resource for help, advice, support, and prayer support for you as a dad. How is the importance of family seen in 2 Timothy 1:5?

Other resources—Have you heard the saying, "A leader is a reader"? Well, it's true! As the leader of your family, be a reader. As a parent, you have numerous resources in books, audio books, video studies, and even your public library or perhaps church library, where many of these resources are available to you free of charge.

Because all of the above resources are available to you as a parent, it's possible for you to go the distance. Now, what is it you need to do as a dad today? What changes need to take place immediately? Start your list here.

3. Choose one of the "Small Steps That Make a Big Difference" and commit to working on it this week. Write it out here, along with some actions you will take right away.

4. What one truth from this chapter had the greatest impact on you as a dad, and why?

How to Study the Bible
—Some Practical Tips

One of the noblest pursuits a child of God can embark upon is to get to know and understand God better. The best way we can accomplish this is to look carefully at the book God has written, the Bible, which communicates who He is and His plan for mankind. There are a number of ways we can study the Bible, but one of the most effective and simple approaches to reading and understanding God's Word involves three simple steps:

> Step 1: Observation—*What does the passage say?*
> Step 2: Interpretation—*What does the passage mean?*
> Step 3: Application—*What am I going to do about what the passage says and means?*

Observation

Observation is the first and most important step in the process. As you read the Bible text, you need to look carefully at what is said, and how it is said. Look for:

- *Terms, not words.* Words can have many meanings, but terms are words used in a specific way in a specific context. (For instance, the word *trunk* could apply to a tree, a car, or a storage box. However, when you read, "That tree has a very large trunk," you know exactly what the word means, which makes it a term.)

- *Structure.* If you look at your Bible, you will see that the text has units called *paragraphs* (indented or marked ¶). A paragraph is a complete unit of thought. You can discover the content of the author's message by noting and understanding each paragraph unit.

▸ *Emphasis.* The amount of space or the number of chapters or verses devoted to a specific topic will reveal the importance of that topic. (For example, note the emphasis of Romans 9–11 and Psalm 119.)

▸ *Repetition.* This is another way an author demonstrates that something is important. One reading of 1 Corinthians 13, where the author uses the word "love" nine times in only 13 verses, communicates to us that love is the focal point of these 13 verses.

▸ *Relationships between ideas.* Pay close attention, for example, to certain relationships that appear in the text:

—Cause-and-effect: "Well done, good and faithful servant; you were faithful over a few things, I will make you ruler over many things" (Matthew 25:21).

—Ifs and thens: "If My people who are called by My name will humble themselves, and pray and seek My face, and turn from their wicked ways, then I will hear from heaven and forgive their sin and heal their land" (2 Chronicles 7:14).

—Questions and answers: "Who is the King of glory? The Lord strong and mighty" (Psalm 24:8).

▸ *Comparisons and contrasts.* For example, "You have heard that it was said…but I say to you…" (Matthew 5:21).

▸ *Literary form.* The Bible is literature, and the three main types of literature in the Bible are discourse (the epistles), prose (Old Testament history), and poetry (the Psalms). Considering the type of literature makes a great deal of difference when you read and interpret the Scriptures.

▸ *Atmosphere.* The author had a particular reason or burden for writing each passage, chapter, and book. Be sure you notice the mood or tone or urgency of the writing.

After you have considered these things, you then are ready to ask the "Wh" questions:

Who?	Who are the people in this passage?
What?	What is happening in this passage?
Where?	Where is this story taking place?
When?	What time (of day, of the year, in history) is it?

Asking these four "Wh" questions can help you notice terms and identify atmosphere. The answers will also enable you to use your imagination to re-create the scene you're reading about.

As you answer the "Wh" questions and imagine the event, you'll probably come up with some questions of your own. Asking those additional questions for understanding will help to build a bridge between observation (the first step) and interpretation (the second step) of the Bible study process.

Interpretation

Interpretation is discovering the meaning of a passage, the author's main thought or idea. Answering the questions that arise during observation will help you in the process of interpretation. Five clues (called "the five C's") can help you determine the author's main point(s):

- ▶ *Context.* You can answer 75 percent of your questions about a passage when you read the text. Reading the text involves looking at the near context (the verse immediately before and after) as well as the far context (the paragraph or the chapter that precedes and/or follows the passage you are studying).

- ▶ *Cross-references.* Let scripture interpret scripture. That is, let other passages in the Bible shed light on the passage you are looking at. At the same time, be careful not to assume that the same word or phrase in two different passages means the same thing.

- ▶ *Culture.* The Bible was written long ago, so when we interpret it, we need to understand it from the writers' cultural context.

- ▶ *Conclusion.* Having answered your questions for understanding by means of context, cross-reference, and culture, you can make a preliminary statement of the passage's meaning. Remember that if your passage consists of more than one paragraph, the author may be presenting more than one thought or idea.

▸ *Consultation.* Reading books known as commentaries, which are written by Bible scholars, can help you interpret Scripture.

Application

Application is why we study the Bible. We want our lives to change. We want to be obedient to God and to grow more like Jesus Christ. After we have observed a passage and interpreted or understood it to the best of our ability, we must then apply its truth to our own life.

You'll want to ask the following questions of every passage of Scripture you study:

▸ How does the truth revealed here affect my relationship with God?

▸ How does this truth affect my relationship with others?

▸ How does this truth affect me?

▸ How does this truth affect my response to the enemy Satan?

The application step is not completed by simply answering these questions. The key is *putting into practice* what God has taught you in your study. Although at any given moment you cannot be consciously applying *every*thing you're learning in Bible study, you can be consciously applying *some*thing. And when you work on applying a truth to your life, God will bless your efforts by, as noted earlier, conforming you to the image of Jesus Christ.

Helpful Bible Study Resources

Concordance—Young's or Strong's
Bible dictionary—Unger's or Holman's
Webster's dictionary
The Zondervan Pictorial Encyclopedia of the Bible
Manners and Customs of the Bible, James M. Freeman

A One-Year
Daily Bible Reading Plan

	Deuteronomy			**1 Samuel**
❑ 19	1–2		❑ 19	1–3
❑ 20	3–4		❑ 20	4–6
❑ 21	5–7		❑ 21	7–9
❑ 22	8–10		❑ 22	10–12
❑ 23	11–13		❑ 23	13–14
❑ 24	14–16		❑ 24	15–16
❑ 25	17–20		❑ 25	17–18
❑ 26	21–23		❑ 26	19–20
❑ 27	24–26		❑ 27	21–23
❑ 28	27–28		❑ 28	24–26
			❑ 29	27–29
			❑ 30	30–31

March

❑ 1	29–30			**2 Samuel**
❑ 2	31–32		❑ 31	1–3
❑ 3	33–34			

Joshua

April

❑ 4	1–4			
❑ 5	5–7		❑ 1	4–6
❑ 6	8–10		❑ 2	7–10
❑ 7	11–14		❑ 3	11–13
❑ 8	15–17		❑ 4	14–15
❑ 9	18–21		❑ 5	16–17
❑ 10	22–24		❑ 6	18–20
			❑ 7	21–22
	Judges		❑ 8	23–24
❑ 11	1–3			
❑ 12	4–6			**1 Kings**
❑ 13	7–9		❑ 9	1–2
❑ 14	10–12		❑ 10	3–5
❑ 15	13–15		❑ 11	6–7
❑ 16	16–18		❑ 12	8–9
❑ 17	19–21		❑ 13	10–12
			❑ 14	13–15
	Ruth		❑ 15	16–18
❑ 18	1–4		❑ 16	19–20
			❑ 17	21–22

2 Kings

❑ 18	1–3
❑ 19	4–6
❑ 20	7–8
❑ 21	9–11
❑ 22	12–14
❑ 23	15–17
❑ 24	18–19
❑ 25	20–22
❑ 26	23–25

1 Chronicles

❑ 27	1–2
❑ 28	3–5
❑ 29	6–7
❑ 30	8–10

May

❑ 1	11–13
❑ 2	14–16
❑ 3	17–19
❑ 4	20–22
❑ 5	23–25
❑ 6	26–27
❑ 7	28–29

2 Chronicles

❑ 8	1–4
❑ 9	5–7
❑ 10	8–10
❑ 11	11–14
❑ 12	15–18
❑ 13	19–21
❑ 14	22–25
❑ 15	26–28
❑ 16	29–31
❑ 17	32–33
❑ 18	34–36

Ezra

❑ 19	1–4
❑ 20	5–7
❑ 21	8–10

Nehemiah

❑ 22	1–3
❑ 23	4–7
❑ 24	8–10
❑ 25	11–13

Esther

❑ 26	1–3
❑ 27	4–7
❑ 28	8–10

Job

❑ 29	1–4
❑ 30	5–8
❑ 31	9–12

June

❑ 1	13–16
❑ 2	17–20
❑ 3	21–24
❑ 4	25–30
❑ 5	31–34
❑ 6	35–38
❑ 7	39–42

Psalms

❑ 8	1–8
❑ 9	9–17
❑ 10	18–21
❑ 11	22–28
❑ 12	29–34
❑ 13	35–39
❑ 14	40–44
❑ 15	45–50

❑ 16	51–56
❑ 17	57–63
❑ 18	64–69
❑ 19	70–74
❑ 20	75–78
❑ 21	79–85
❑ 22	86–90
❑ 23	91–98
❑ 24	99–104
❑ 25	105–107
❑ 26	108–113
❑ 27	114–118
❑ 28	119
❑ 29	120–134
❑ 30	135–142

July

| ❑ 1 | 143–150 |

Proverbs

❑ 2	1–3
❑ 3	4–7
❑ 4	8–11
❑ 5	12–15
❑ 6	16–18
❑ 7	19–21
❑ 8	22–24
❑ 9	25–28
❑ 10	29–31

Ecclesiastes

❑ 11	1–4
❑ 12	5–8
❑ 13	9–12

Song of Solomon

| ❑ 14 | 1–4 |
| ❑ 15 | 5–8 |

Isaiah

❑ 16	1–4
❑ 17	5–8
❑ 18	9–12
❑ 19	13–15
❑ 20	16–20
❑ 21	21–24
❑ 22	25–28
❑ 23	29–32
❑ 24	33–36
❑ 25	37–40
❑ 26	41–43
❑ 27	44–46
❑ 28	47–49
❑ 29	50–52
❑ 30	53–56
❑ 31	57–60

August

| ❑ 1 | 61–63 |
| ❑ 2 | 64–66 |

Jeremiah

❑ 3	1–3
❑ 4	4–6
❑ 5	7–9
❑ 6	10–12
❑ 7	13–15
❑ 8	16–19
❑ 9	20–22
❑ 10	23–25
❑ 11	26–29
❑ 12	30–31
❑ 13	32–34
❑ 14	35–37
❑ 15	38–40
❑ 16	41–44
❑ 17	45–48
❑ 18	49–50

❏ 19	51–52		❏ 15	**Joel**
	Lamentations			**Amos**
❏ 20	1–2		❏ 16	1–4
❏ 21	3–5		❏ 17	5–9
	Ezekiel		❏ 18	**Obadiah** and **Jonah**
❏ 22	1–4			
❏ 23	5–8			**Micah**
❏ 24	9–12		❏ 19	1–4
❏ 25	13–15		❏ 20	5–7
❏ 26	16–17			
❏ 27	18–20		❏ 21	**Nahum**
❏ 28	21–23			
❏ 29	24–26		❏ 22	**Habakkuk**
❏ 30	27–29			
❏ 31	30–31		❏ 23	**Zephaniah**

September

			❏ 24	**Haggai**
❏ 1	32–33			
❏ 2	34–36			**Zechariah**
❏ 3	37–39		❏ 25	1–4
❏ 4	40–42		❏ 26	5–9
❏ 5	43–45		❏ 27	10–14
❏ 6	46–48			
			❏ 28	**Malachi**
	Daniel			
❏ 7	1–2			**Matthew**
❏ 8	3–4		❏ 29	1–4
❏ 9	5–6		❏ 30	5–7
❏ 10	7–9			
❏ 11	10–12			

October

	Hosea		❏ 1	8–9
❏ 12	1–4		❏ 2	10–11
❏ 13	5–9		❏ 3	12–13
❏ 14	10–14		❏ 4	14–16
			❏ 5	17–18

❑ 6	19–20
❑ 7	21–22
❑ 8	23–24
❑ 9	25–26
❑ 10	27–28

Mark

❑ 11	1–3
❑ 12	4–5
❑ 13	6–7
❑ 14	8–9
❑ 15	10–11
❑ 16	12–13
❑ 17	14
❑ 18	15–16

Luke

❑ 19	1–2
❑ 20	3–4
❑ 21	5–6
❑ 22	7–8
❑ 23	9–10
❑ 24	11–12
❑ 25	13–14
❑ 26	15–16
❑ 27	17–18
❑ 28	19–20
❑ 29	21–22
❑ 30	23–24

John

| ❑ 31 | 1–3 |

❑ 4	10–11
❑ 5	12–13
❑ 6	14–16
❑ 7	17–19
❑ 8	20–21

Acts

❑ 9	1–3
❑ 10	4–5
❑ 11	6–7
❑ 12	8–9
❑ 13	10–11
❑ 14	12–13
❑ 15	14–15
❑ 16	16–17
❑ 17	18–19
❑ 18	20–21
❑ 19	22–23
❑ 20	24–26
❑ 21	27–28

Romans

❑ 22	1–3
❑ 23	4–6
❑ 24	7–9
❑ 25	10–12
❑ 26	13–14
❑ 27	15–16

1 Corinthians

❑ 28	1–4
❑ 29	5–7
❑ 30	8–10

November

❑ 1	4–5
❑ 2	6–7
❑ 3	8–9

December

| ❑ 1 | 11–13 |
| ❑ 2 | 14–16 |

2 Corinthians
- ❏ 3   1–4
- ❏ 4   5–9
- ❏ 5   10–13

Galatians
- ❏ 6   1–3
- ❏ 7   4–6

Ephesians
- ❏ 8   1–3
- ❏ 9   4–6

- ❏ 10   **Philippians**

- ❏ 11   **Colossians**

- ❏ 12   **1 Thessalonians**

- ❏ 13   **2 Thessalonians**

- ❏ 14   **1 Timothy**

- ❏ 15   **2 Timothy**

- ❏ 16   **Titus** and **Philemon**

Hebrews
- ❏ 17   1–4
- ❏ 18   5–8
- ❏ 19   9–10
- ❏ 20   11–13

- ❏ 21   **James**

- ❏ 22   **1 Peter**

- ❏ 23   **2 Peter**

- ❏ 24   **1 John**

- ❏ 25   **2, 3 John, Jude**

Revelation
- ❏ 26   1–3
- ❏ 27   4–8
- ❏ 28   9–12
- ❏ 29   13–16
- ❏ 30   17–19
- ❏ 31   20–22

Notes

From a Dad's Heart

1. *A Boy After God's Own Heart* (Eugene, OR: Harvest House, 2012), and *A Young Man After God's Own Heart* (Eugene, OR: Harvest House, 2005).

Chapter 1—A Dad Who Has a Divine Model

1. William Barclay, as cited in Albert M. Wells, Jr., ed., *Inspiring Quotations, Contemporary and Classical* (Nashville, TN: Thomas Nelson, 1988), p. 71.
2. John Drescher, as cited in Wells, *Inspiring Quotations,* p. 71.

Chapter 2—A Dad Who Walks in the Spirit

1. John MacArthur, Jr., *Liberty in Christ* (Panorama City, CA: Word of Grace Communications, 1986), p. 88.
2. This quote is famously attributed to John Wesley, but there are sources that state it cannot be found in his writings.
3. Source unknown.
4. Attributed to George Herbert, but source unknown.

Chapter 3—A Dad Who Is a Teacher

1. Ruth Vaughan, as cited in Albert M. Wells, Jr., ed., *Inspiring Quotations, Contemporary and Classical* (Nashville, TN: Thomas Nelson, 1988), p. 196.
2. *Matthew Henry's Commentary on the Whole Bible* (Hendrickson, 1991), p. 244.
3. *Matthew Henry's Commentary on the Whole Bible,* p. 244.
4. As cited in Wells, Jr., ed., *Inspiring Quotations,* p. 119.
5. Tedd Tripp, *Shepherding a Child's Heart* (Wapwallopen, PA: Shepherd Press, 1995), p. 33.
6. Jim George, *A Husband After God's Own Heart* (Eugene OR: Harvest House, 2004), p. 111.
7. *Our Daily Bread* (Grand Rapids, MI: Radio Bible Class, 1980), September 18.

Chapter 4—A Dad Who Is a Trainer

1. C.H. Spurgeon, *Come Ye Children* (London: Passmore & Alabaster, 1897), opening of chapter 8.
2. Attributed to Benjamin Franklin, source unknown.

Chapter 5—A Dad Who Is an Instructor

1. Sir Alexander Paterson, as cited in Albert M. Wells, Jr., ed., *Inspiring Quotations, Contemporary and Classical* (Nashville, TN: Thomas Nelson, 1988), p. 58.

2. *A Man After God's Own Heart* (Eugene, OR: Harvest House, 2002); *A Husband After God's Own Heart* (Eugene, OR: Harvest House, 2004); *A Young Man After God's Own Heart* (Eugene, OR: Harvest House, 2005); *A Boy After God's Own Heart* (Eugene, OR: Harvest House, 2012); *A Leader After God's Own Heart* (Eugene, OR: Harvest House, 2012).

3. Sir Alexander Paterson, as cited in Wells, Jr., ed., *Inspiring Quotations*, p. 58.

Chapter 6—A Dad Who Is an Intercessor

1. Merrill C. Tenney, as cited in Paul Lee Tan, *Encyclopedia of 7,700 Illustrations* (Winona Lake, IN: BMH Books, 1979), p. 434.

2. Jim George, *The Man Who Makes a Difference* (Eugene OR: Harvest House, 2010), pp. 58-60.

3. This saying is attributed to Leonard Ravenhill, British evangelist, 1907–1994.

Chapter 7—A Dad Who Is a Prayer Warrior

1. C.H. Spurgeon, *Sermons of the Rev. C.H. Spurgeon*, First Series (New York: Sheldon, Blakeman, 1857), p. 183.

2. *Life Application Bible* (Wheaton IL: Tyndale House, 1988), p. 864.

3. Martin Luther, as cited in Albert M. Wells, Jr., ed., *Inspiring Quotations, Contemporary and Classical* (Nashville, TN: Thomas Nelson, 1988), p. 159.

4. Elizabeth George, *A Little Girl After God's Own Heart* (Eugene, OR: Harvest House, 2000).

5. Louis H. Evans as cited in Wells, Jr., ed., *Inspiring Quotations*, p. 159.

Chapter 9—A Dad Who Is a Watchman

1. Burce B. Barton, ed., *Life Application Bible Commentary—Acts* (Wheaton, IL: Tyndale House, 1999), p. 349.

2. See Romans 1:9-10; Ephesians 1:15-16; Philippians 1:4; 1 Thessalonians 1:2-3; 2 Thessalonians 1:11; 2 Timothy 1:3; Philemon 4.

3. See 1 Thessalonians 2:13; 2 Timothy 3:16-17; 2 Peter 3:18.

Chapter 10—A Dad Who Is a Guide

1. Joseph Addison as cited in Albert M. Wells, Jr., ed., *Inspiring Quotations, Contemporary and Classical* (Nashville, TN: Thomas Nelson, 1988), p. 168.

2. Jim George, *A Man After God's Own Heart* (Eugene OR: Harvest House, 2002), p. 142.

3. Bruce B. Barton, *Life Application Bible Commentary—1 Timothy, 2 Timothy, Titus* (Wheaton, IL: Tyndale House, 1993), p. 192.

Chapter 11—A Dad Who Is an Encourager

1. Henry Drummond, *The Greatest Thing in the World* (Boston: International Pocket Library, 1936), p. 21.

2. Charles R. Swindoll, *Insight for Living* radio broadcast, March 26, 2008.

Chapter 12—A Dad Who Is a Team Player

1. Cited in *The Henry Ford, 2004 Annual Report* (Dearborn, MI: The Henry Ford, 2004).

Chapter 13—A Dad Who Goes the Distance

1. From Charles R. Swindoll's book *Growing Strong in the Season of Life*, as cited in *Lists to Live By*, compiled by Alice Gray, Steve Stephens, John Van Diest (Sisters, OR: Multnomah, 1999), p. 267.

Study Guide

1. Bruce B. Barton et al, *Life Application Bible Commentary—Luke* (Wheaton, IL: Tyndale House, 1997), p. 56.
2. Charles F. Phfeiffer and Everett F. Harrison, eds., *The Wycliffe Bible Commentary* (Chicago, IL: Moody Press, 1973), p. 5.

Other Books by Jim George

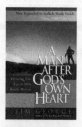

A Man After God's Own Heart
Many Christian men want to be men after God's own heart...but how do they do this? George shows that a heartfelt desire to practice God's priorities is all that's needed. God's grace does the rest.

A Man After God's Own Heart Devotional
This book is filled with quick, focused devotions that will encourage your spiritual growth, equip you to persevere when life gets tough, manage your responsibilities well with wisdom, and live with maximum impact in all you do.

A Husband After God's Own Heart
You'll find your marriage growing richer and deeper as you pursue God and discover 12 areas in which you can make a real difference in your relationship with your wife.

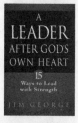

A Leader After God's Own Heart
Every man is either a leader or a leader in the making—whether at work, in the home, or any other setting. So what does it take to be a good leader—one God can use? This book will equip you to lead with strength and have a positive, lasting impact.

The Man Who Makes a Difference
How can you have a lasting impact? Here are the secrets to having a positive and meaningful influence in the lives of everyone you meet, including your wife and children.

A Young Man After God's Own Heart

Pursuing God really is an adventure—a lot like climbing a mountain. There are many challenges on the way up, but the great view at the top is well worth the trip. This book helps young men to experience the thrill of knowing real success in life—the kind that counts with God.

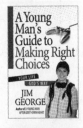

A Young Man's Guide to Making Right Choices

This book will help teen guys to think carefully about their decisions, assuring they gain the skills needed to face life's challenges.

The Bare Bones Bible® Handbook

The perfect resource for a fast and friendly overview of every book of the Bible. Excellent for anyone who wants to know the Bible better and get more from their interaction with God's Word.

The Bare Bones Bible® Handbook for Teens

Based on the bestselling Bare Bones Bible® Handbook, this edition includes content and life applications specially written with teens in mind. They will be amazed at how much the Bible has to say about the things that matter most to them.

10 Minutes to Knowing the Men and Women of the Bible

The lessons you can learn from the outstanding men and women of the Bible are powerfully relevant for today. As you review their lives, you'll discover special qualities worth emulating and life lessons for everyday living.

Know Your Bible from A to Z

This is a concise, easy-to-understand A-to-Z survey of the Bible's most important people, places, customs, and events. A great help for understanding the big picture of the Bible and applying the Scriptures to your daily life.

A Boy After God's Own Heart

This book helps boys learn how to make good decisions and great friends, see the benefits of homework and chores, get along better with their parents and siblings, and get into the Bible and grow closer to God.

A Boy's Guide to Making Really Good Choices

Making good choices is the biggest step a boy can take toward growing up. This book helps boys learn to make the best kinds of choices—those that make them stronger, wiser, and more mature.

God Loves His Precious Children
(coauthored with Elizabeth George)
Jim and Elizabeth George share the comfort and assurance of Psalm 23 with young children. Engaging watercolor scenes by artist Judy Luenebrink and delightful rhymes by Jim and Elizabeth bring the truths of each verse to life.

God's Wisdom for Little Boys
(coauthored with Elizabeth George)
The wonderful teachings of Proverbs come to life for boys. Memorable rhymes play alongside colorful paintings for a charming presentation of truths to live by.